Awesome Real Estate Strategies

Creating Wealth Investing in Real Estate

Shawn M. Tennefoss

Awesome Real Estate Strategies

Written by Shawn M. Tennefoss

Printed in the United States of America

Author: Shawn M. Tennefoss

Foreword by Jeff Kaller

First Printing

Disclaimer:

All real estate investments involve different degrees of risk. You should be acutely aware of your financial status and risk tolerance level at all times. Furthermore, you should read all agreements, contracts, documents and representations carefully before making any investment decisions. You are free at all times to accept, reject or stipulate any and all investment recommendations made by the author. All real estate Investments and strategies presented by the author are subject to market risk and may result in the entire loss to the client's investment.

Please understand that any losses are attributed to market forces beyond the control or prediction of the author. As you know, any Real Estate strategy recommendation, which you are free to accept, reject or stipulate to, is not a guarantee for the successful performance of said investment.

The information contained herein should not be used in any actual transaction without the advice and guidance of a professional 'Tax Advisor' who is familiar with all the relevant facts. The information contained in any potential real estate investment is general in nature and is not intended as legal, tax or investment advice.

Furthermore, said information may not be applicable to or suitable for the individuals' specific circumstances or financial needs and may require consideration of other matters. The document originator assumes no obligation to inform any person of any changes in the law or other factors that could affect the information contained herein. The information contained herein is written without warranty and reader should consult an attorney if at any time they have questions beyond the scope of this text.

TABLE OF CONTENTS

Foreword

It is my privilege to write this foreword for Shawn M. Tennefoss. As a 20 year veteran myself, investing in distressed Real Estate, countless hours as a personal coach, and mentor for thousands of students within the short sale arena, I have known many who continued on to great success. Shawn is one of them! In his dynamic book, Shawn shares his strategies and systems, including short sales, in a way that everyone can grasp and get a good overview of each technique.

It's interesting that after being involved in 1,000 transactions, my wife Sofia and I have learned the importance of technique and a formulaic approach. Shawn has this nailed. Beyond how you communicate, is another, even more important component; Sure Shawn has proven technical expertise in construction and negotiation; moreover, it's about how Shawn approaches his work with integrity and enthusiasm, in keeping with his philosophy about real estate investment as a great way to make an honest profit and his desire to do work of real worth.

I'm very enthusiastic about this new book, whether it's Shawn's knowledge of fixing up single family houses for profit or his insights about analyzing a potential multi-family property, it will aide in bringing clarity to your decision making process. You'll learn when to buy and when to walk away. Once you understand these concepts, you won't want to buy another property without implementing one or more of these Awesome Real Estate strategies.

Having a step by step process is very important, whether you are going to fix and flip, buy and hold or simply work deals to wholesale to others. Through these systems you will find a useful and meaningful way to help others and create profit for yourself and your family.

Following these techniques will allow you to make more money. The other half is the uncanny way that this book will instill confidence to do well and do it with integrity. You will begin to recognize that every time you close a deal you are solving an issue for someone or even a family. My group has collectively help more than one million begrudged families from losing their homes to foreclosure. It all started with the decision to take action and get educated that has led me to achievements that have reached people at levels that I never would have expected. I ask this one question to you: What are you capable of? You will never know unless you pick up the ball and run with it. Helping others in the spirit of service, while liberating your own life…sounds like a pretty great place. Now it's your turn for this to become your real estate investing reality.

Shawn is one such person and since that time he has taken the bull by the horns and made a successful career from Real Estate investing.   He is the only person I know that took his investing carrier to the road and saw the country all the while running a successful real estate business. Enjoy Reading this dynamite book and learning from my friend Shawn, who truly gets it; investing and living a balanced life!   Enjoy Awesome Real Estate Strategies!

To your explosive success,

Jeff Kaller

(Aka Mr. Preforeclosure)

Preface and Acknowledgments

The information you hold in your hands is a collection of some of the best Real Estate strategies I have been using personally with great success, (truly awesome techniques). This book has been written using the information and experiences I have gathered over the years through tens of thousands of dollars in education expense and business losses to derive a group of systems that I believe are the key to success in the Real Estate business. They have made me a lot of money and I know they will do the same for you. It hasn't been easy but, once I got onto these key systems, that work, I have pursued them with fervor.

At one time, I was taking all the profits from any given short sale or construction project and spending them to increase the size of my house, buy a fancier car, purchase a second home and on, and on and on it went. Using the money from the flips and sales to pay payments on non-income producing assets is foolish at best. It a recipe for disaster!

First hurricane Katrina hit all of our properties in New Orleans, stopping any money from sales there for a while. Then the economy took a nose dive, stopping any chance of selling our vacation house in Oregon or our investment properties in Florida and other states. This very efficiently stopped our ability to make the payments on all those goodies. We took every dime we had in retirement, savings and operating accounts to make payments. *What a waste of good money! (Throwing good money after bad, as they say).* Since our income was based on the equity we had in those houses and dependent on sales, we had nothing!

Fortunately my wife and I are fighters, so we wrangled, squirmed, negotiated and used any angle we could find to get the debts and the properties off our backs. It took almost 3-4 years, if you can believe that, but after that, we had liquidated everything without any foreclosures or bankruptcy. Most importantly without a divorce! These types of situations can ruin a marriage; however my wife has been with me every step of the way for almost 30 years and this was no exception. She hung in there and now we can enjoy building our future together, the right way, to include security and freedom!

I tell you this so you will understand that I am speaking from experience and that my knowledge of short-sales, negotiations, private capital and creative financing actually saved "my bacon" when it was needed. I started with nothing, built a successful Real Estate business and these unfortunate experiences cost me everything, but now you can use my personal "education opportunities" to further yourself and save your hard earned money! We did have to start over though, and this time it was using the techniques I talk about here. This is a priceless gathering of information for you to use that will cost you a small amount of time and the cost of this book, but will pay you back dividends for years to come. **To your Prosperity!**

Chapter One

Rehabbing

"You always pass failure on the way to success!" Mickey Rooney

I t seems only appropriate to start this book where I started, rehabbing. Many successful real estate investors that I know got their start as "Rehabbers".

One of the most important things you can learn before you buy an Investment Property of any kind is the following:

You make your money when you buy!

Let me restate that:

You make your money on any given property when you purchase the property, not when you sell the property. So please take the time to find a low enough price to actually have a profit when you are done with the rehab.

I've been an active real estate investor for the past 10-12 years. Prior to that I had either remodeled or participated in construction projects helping other investors obtain their dreams.

I've seen projects go over budget, and investors lose their "proverbial butt".   Most of these mistakes could have been avoided by making advanced preparations and estimates before investing in the project.

Since this book is focused on real estate strategies and not how to succeed in the construction business I'm going to go into general information on rehabbing not specific information on construction management or running a construction company.
I will tell you however, that even though we use a lot of different ways to buy and sell Real estate, I still use Rehabbing as one of my major revenue sources. As I've mentioned earlier in a chapter, the biggest lesson you can learn before you buy anything is to buy low enough... you make your profit when you buy, not when you sell!

Let's go over this idea in a little better detail:
If you know the market (selling price) for any given house is, for example: $200,000.00 move-in ready, then you want to be selling yours for say $180,000-$190,000 or about 10%-15% below your comparables, so it does not sit on the market like so many houses. This means that you will need to take the cost of the house, plus the cost of construction, plus the cost of realtors' fees, plus the closing costs, plus any taxes, plus a return for your investor and finally a return for yourself so you make money.   (That is why we

are doing this, right?!?). If you use a bank, then add in the interest cost or (your holding costs), if you use private money or "hard" money (cash) then add that cost in.

In this chapter, we're going to go over some specific numbers and a couple of real life examples on houses that we have bought and sold.   For now let's get started on the nuts and bolts of rehabbing step by step.

- First let's estimate what our rehab will cost:

OK, so you've found a house. You want to purchase it for a cheap enough price that you know you can make money when you sell it. (Remember when you buy, not when you sell!)   Now comes the hard part. *Estimating the cost of repairs.*   The first thing I do when I walk through a house is look at the four largest items, or the "BIG FOUR", as I like to call them. Roof, mechanical, electrical, and plumbing. Secondly I look at the cosmetic items. These are the ones that scare most of the people away but are actually the most straight forward to work with. Since I replace the kitchens and bathrooms in almost every house I buy, I already know what they cost. You will have to take the time to figure your actual costs the first few times, so you can simply look past the kitchen and baths and already know that you will be replacing them. This will allow you to focus on the items I mentioned above.

Kitchens and baths. As long as you are not changing the actual shape of the rooms, or the shape of the kitchen cabinet layout, it is actually quite simple.   You remove the old cabinets and put in new ones that look better. Add granite and a tile back splash and viola' you've got a great looking house again!

So take the following steps to calculate your costs on all your future projects.

1) Go to Home Depot or Lowes. (Orange or Blue, your choice) Find a cabinet that most folks will like. Get a cost on four or five size kitchens, such as a 10' X10' and a 10' X 12' and a 14'X 12', etc. This will give you your "basis" for estimating your first cost.

2) Add misc. cabinets that will fill in the space for the specific kitchen your doing on a particular house. Such as a tall pantry cabinet may add $350 or a row of base cabinets for a breakfast bar may add $1200. That way when you look at the new project house, you will measure the kitchen, plug in your cabinet costs plus misc. cabinets and viola' your first line item on your estimate.

3) Add you cost of granite counters. I know that my costs are always between $1500 -$2000 depending on the size. Including a small 4" backsplash. I look at craigslist.com and call two or three granite guys and let them know I buy several houses per year and would like to get a quote on

counters to use as I buy houses. It may take you talking to four or five guys but someone will want to earn your business and give you a great price. The folks I use are reasonable and reliable and the solid granite adds waaaay more value than it costs me. If possible, use the solid slab, not the tiles. It will give you back tenfold when you sell the house.

4) If you want to make the house look even higher-end, then add tumbled marble above the granite backsplash. This is an easy line item to estimate since you can simply add the space between the cabinets and the length, this will give you your square footage, then take the cost per square foot, such as $5.50 per square foot, times say, 200 square feet, equals $1,000.

If you do nothing else but carefully inspect the first four items, (plus kitchens and baths) it will make you money every single time. Also, know how much an "appliance package" costs.

Inspect the Roof: Now if you're not a person that likes to take out ladders and start climbing around on top of roofs or maybe the roof is too high for your ladder, then by all means call a roofer and ask for an estimate.   Make sure to talk with the roofer and let them know you are an investor who will be buying several houses per year and you would like to be able to call them when you are estimating a house re-hab. It took me probably ten guys to find a good roofer, so keep trying until you find someone you like to work with. You will probably replace one in ten roofs on re-habs but that one in ten can be expensive, if you are not aware of it. I have found that sometimes, just replacing the gutters and downspouts makes a huge difference on the looks of the house.

Structure: I include the exterior paint, trim and items such as the fascia, etc in this category. Take the time to walk around the property looking for cracks in the foundation or under the corners of the windows. If you've got a structural problem, it's expensive, anywhere from $7500 to $30,000 to repair and could kill your deal. If the house needs paint, you should have a good idea of the costs to paint the outside of a house in your neighborhood. I have two guys that work for me full time and they do all the painting but I still have to know how many hours and how much paint it will take to caulk and paint the house outside.

Plumbing: Start by taking a look under the sinks in the kitchens and bathrooms; closely examine the drains and water supply lines for signs of rust or cracks or shoddy repairs and workmanship. It's common to find bad connections, missing garbage disposals, etc. Just make sure to add these things into your estimate so they don't surprise you.

I have added an inspection form on

www.awesomerealestatestrategies.com , go down load it and use

it or change it to fit your system. Take a look at the bottom of the

showers and around each toilet.   Take the time to step right next

to each toilet with your foot and feel if the floor is soft.   In

Florida, we use mainly concrete floors, (and cbs framing), so this is

usually not an issue, but in New Orleans and Oregon where I buy

and sell houses too, we have wood framed floors, so check them

for soft spots and damage.

Finally, turn on the water in each and every sink, tub and flush

each toilet. Watch the water go down the drain, does it take a

long time? Does it look rusty? Does it clog up entirely? If each and

every drain and toilet goes slow, it may be a main drain line

problem, if it's only one fixture, probably just a bad pee trap or

similar. If you want to pay for the $300 drain line video, do that. I

only add that expense, if I see a potential issue.

Next, how is the water pressure?   Are the water supply pipes

made of galvanized pipes? These can plug up and create a real

hassle. You may want o have a plumber look at the main line if

you want the house but the supply lines are in question.

I could write an entire book on the re-habbing side of the business

but this is really about your real estate investing business and

using different strategies for each house you buy. Re-habbing is just one of many strategies I use. However, I want you to be hugely successful with your business, so I go into detail to ensure your success.

Electrical system: Find the breaker box. (Used to be called a "fuse box" since fuses were used in the past).   Learn the difference between breakers and fuses. Which does this house have? Was the system ever upgraded?   Look at the Air conditioning and heating unit. If it's a central unit, find the date on the sticker on both the inside unit, (the handler) and the outside unit, (the condenser). This will tell you the approx. date it was manufactured, it is usually installed within a year of that sticker date. AS far as the rest of the electrical system, I always recommend getting an electrician to check out the house, if you think things looks like they are "cobbled together". Buy yourself a small plug in tester at the hardware store.   You can plug this in in each room to see if each plug in is grounded. That is usually a good indication of the wiring.

Also, Tile or carpet?   Depending on the area and demographics folks prefer one or the other. I prefer tile in most areas and wood floors everywhere else. You have to know your given market. Always figure you'll have to paint inside and outside and do some minor landscaping.   It will depend on your exit strategy for each house. Look at the surrounding houses.   Make sure you are not the nicest house on the street. You don't want to be a "trail blazer". That's a fast way to go broke.

If you break it down like this after a while you'll know what things cost and you can estimate repairs before rehabbing or consider wholesaling it to another investor.   If you also want to sell it to another investor it will be to your advantage to know what the costs are and the repairs that are needed to Inform an investor of those repairs. I give the full estimate sheet to other investors when I wholesale a property. They love this, since they have a great idea of the costs.

2. Working with Hired Help.

There are two ways to rehab: do it yourself or hire someone. (I'm sure there are more than two ways!)   There are pros and cons to both.   If you can do it, you save money on labor.   The downside is that while you are working on your re-hab, you are not out bidding on houses and working on your business.   If you have a day job, this limits you to nights and weekends.   It can take several extra months. I can tell you that I did all my own work on the first few houses. Then hired a few sub-contractors, then eventually hired workers. I am a good manager of people and that is very important if you hire help. Subs can be good since they get paid on results.

With hired help, you have the cost of labor; and you have to make sure that they do a good job; but they can do it in a lot less time than it would take you.   That means you sell it faster and move on to next house.   It will also make because you're holding costs to be considerably less. Now, I only work with contractors and labor.

If I have to use someone that I do not know, I always give them a smaller project and more supervision to see how they do and then move them up to larger jobs and less supervision.   If they don't do well, don't use them again.   We currently have two crews and we pay them well.   Getting doughnuts and coffee for them is a nice gesture when you stop by in the morning.   Since we mainly work in warm climates, I try to bring sports drinks or ice water around lunchtime or mid-afternoon to keep up spirits and work strength.   I believe you must inspect the properties daily yourself. One of my biggest mistakes and hence learning lessons has been that you cannot trust anyone to take care of your business they way you would.   They can be the best at their jobs but they are not you and this is not their business or project... Every morning I try to meet the crew at the job site.   This ensures that they arrive on time and that they have the supplies that they need to complete their work for the day.   Since I hire my own workers, I give them an hourly wage and then bring the supplies as they need them.   I like to give a small bonus to the guys when the house is finished if they have kept to a budget and worked steady. I find that the more I can be there to check things out, the better and more smoothly the project goes.   This is why you need to stay on top of them each day.

3. Buying Supplies

Unless you live next door to Home Depot or Lowe's, pay your workers a bit extra to help you get the supplies.   Unfortunately, it is not uncommon to make four or five trips daily to get supplies. Since my workers get paid by the hour, I have them meet me at the supply store in the morning sometimes. Get them started gathering sheetrock and loading the carts. Or sometimes, I give them a list the night before and have them go to the store in the morning and start loading the carts, then I meet them there and pay. Have them load the truck, unload the truck and start working. I can always be making calls while they are loading the carts, the truck, etc.

Tip: When we have several projects going at one time, we give

each one of our project managers a gift card from Home Depot or Lowe's.   They give us all the receipts, then when they run out of money on the cards, you buy them another card.   We pay them a bit extra to get the supplies they need.   Since they've been working for us for a while now, we can trust them.

If the workers cannot get the supplies, we make the trips ourselves.   We prefer to focus on acquiring more properties. If the properties are 50 miles apart, you have the travel time to consider.

 Make sure you keep separate invoices and receipts for each property. When I get supplies for two or three properties, I have to get separate receipts. It may not seem too important until tax time or when you need to know your exact costs. Your accountant and bookkeeper will thank you.

4. Securing the property

When you are rehabbing a house, take the time to cover each of the windows with either newspaper or some type of plastic that you cannot see through from the outside.   Keep the doors closed in the front when you are working.   Take the signs off your car when you are there since the only ones who will talk to you are folks who will waste your time.   The time for signs and showing off the place is after it is finished. Keep the music down or off and make your workers do the same.   The last thing you need is a neighbor who is upset calling the city on you. The code enforcement department can be a real pain.   Also, don't ever let them in the house.   Talk to them in the driveway.   If you have a permit violation or a code violation, "you will get it taken care of", just be smart enough to not let them find any more, which they usually will, if given the chance.   I have had people come into houses I was redoing and actually take out the ceiling fans, hot water heaters, tear open the walls and steal the copper pipes! Take a few extra steps to secure the side gates. Leave a car in the driveway if possible. Leave a hall light on, turn on a radio in the kitchen on a talk show. One time they took the water heaters and just left the pipes running in the middle of the house. What a mess! You will thank yourself later for a little precaution now.

5. City Building Permits

Get permits if you are required to do so...   You will really need them for structures, roofs, electrical and plumbing.   In most areas even for windows.   The cost is not usually that high and when you re-sell the house, you will be glad you got them and everything is "above board". Some things you can do yourself on your own over a weekend and possibly avoid permits but you are playing roulette. I don't advocate one way or the other; you will weigh your own risks. I can tell you that after the first time a potential buyer walks away from your freshly remodeled house due to no permits on file from the city, you will reconsider not filing for permits over losing a sale or potential buyer. I have no problem, painting, replacing kitchen cabinets or adding tile without permits. Anything else, please get them and save your future sale.

6. For Sale!

One of the big questions that come up when talking to investors about doing rehabs is:

When is the best time to start advertising the place for sale?

Sign in the yard during rehab?

Listing on the MLS?

I prefer to wait until the house is almost finished before I put a sign in the yard. I have had buyers see the house early with all the plumbing cut off and the wires hanging down from the ceiling and no cabinets and they have walked away. Just because you have imagination does not mean that everyone does. In fact, most folks do not have the ability to visualize a project that is why they buy houses from us!

Most of the potential buyers will not make an offer that is reasonable if they see the house before completion.   The challenges of trying to sell a house with a crew working inside and construction debris everywhere is not worth the trouble.   It wastes your time and the time of the crew who has to stop making noise for the hour or so people are walking around.

One technique we use when selling a house is to deliver post cards or a letter to each of the neighboring houses offering them a $300 referral fee if they send a friend to buy the house. Most folks want to live by people they like and everyone likes to make money!   It costs very little to produce the cards, in fact we print them on our laser printer and stick them to the doors or hand them to the homeowners.   (Do not put them in the mailbox, it is illegal).

 See sample letter below:

Dear Neighbor,

We just purchased the home at _____ and absolutely love your neighborhood!   Only, we have a problem; the home needs a new owner and we thought you could help.

We thought you might know of a family member or friend who

would want the first chance before we put the house out on the market to just anybody.   We're happy to pay a referral fee and can offer anyone you know a discount who buys the house.

It's our way of saying how important it is to help maintain the integrity of your neighborhood.   Our company offers a variety of ways to help buyers to purchase a home including Owner Financing.

If it ends up being immediate family member, we could even make two of their first house payments.   This is our way of saying thanks.

Warmly,

Your Name
Your Company
XXX-XXXX

P.S. Don't forget to put your name and number on the bottom of this page so we know who to do something nice for.

P.S.S. Remember, for any close friends in or out of state, now is the time to see if you can get them to move closer.

✄ --

Name: _____

Phone: _____

Tip: I keep a clip board that hangs on the front door and if someone stops by who is interested in the house, I have them

put their name and number on a list and we call them when it is available to be shown. It usually provides a few good leads. *"I am always ready to learn although I do not always like being taught!"* Winston Churchill.

7. Negotiating with the Realtors and Homeowners.

Usually there is enough room in a deal to work with a Realtor who has a buyer. I do not list my property with Realtors as a general rule. I have no problem paying a Realtor 3% for a buyer who is qualified. Note that I said "who is qualified". Most will tell you that they have a buyer for you. However, if they have not taken the time to get that "buyer" qualified, then they are not a "buyer". In other words, if you don't know how much you have in your pocket to spend then you cannot buy anything. It is very important you try not to tie up your house with someone who has not taken the time to get a loan. Also, as far as the MLS is concerned, I pay a flat fee to list my properties. It only cost a few hundred dollars and I can keep track of the sales process directly... After all, the selling of the house is one of the most important things you will be dong in the process.

I learned about selling my own houses a while ago. I can think of so many times that a buyer wanted the house but the agent (Realtor) did not ask the important questions. Do yourself a favor and add the following sentences to your vocabulary:

A. **On a scale of 1-10 with 1 being, you did not like the house and 10 being the house is perfect, what number are you at?** Now, it does not matter what number they pick. The magic is in the next question and I highly suggest you write it down and commit it to memory: **WHAT WOULD IT TAKE TO GET YOU TO A 10?**

Once they tell you what their concerns are, you have a chance to address their concerns. They may say, well the paint is ugly and the gutters are sagging in the back. You could easily answer what if I painted the color of your choice and replaced the gutters? However, if you do not ask, like most people, you will never know what they would think about it. Sometimes they just do not like the house and there is nothing you can do or at least can afford to do but it is always a good idea to find out. I learned this from Anthony (Tony) Robbins who has so many strategic and important ways to use language to get to your goals. I highly recommend learning some of his techniques and especially his attitude towards your life!

When you do have a buyer, you need to speak to the mortgage broker if possible. They need to be approved and you want them to be able to close within 30-45 days or less. In the purchase contract you should have a clause that gives them 5-7 days to get a pre-approval letter to you so you can either move to another buyer or find a different mortgage broker for them.

I usually do not list my houses.   About 20% of my buyers are represented by agents, but the agents didn't bring the buyers to my house, the buyers bring the agent.   I do a co-op with these agents.   (Pay a 3% commission or sometimes less).

I don't negotiate with the buyers, at least not in the conventional sense. Since we already know that we bought the house well below market and have it priced below current comparables, then why negotiate too much?   I get calls from prospects when a house is completed.   I hold 1-2 hour open houses on the first two Saturdays or Sundays.   We call every prospect to tell them about the open houses, then list the open houses in our flyers, craigslist.com and a sign we stick in the yard and several signs on directional corners.

We will usually have about 15-20 prospects call and about 5-7 will show up at the first open house and a couple more of those at the second open house.   9 times out of 10 one of them will buy the house.   If a buyer has completed one of our loan application packets or forms and their credit looks OK, then we don't mind putting it under contract.   We do not make them wait until after the open house.   We jump right in with them.

If we have a buyer ready to buy a house and nothing is finished yet, we try and show them a house we have just completed, so they can feel comfortable with us.   I hope you noticed that we call a buyer, a buyer, not a prospect once they have made the commitment to buy and have been qualified. Showing them a finished house will "wet their appetite" so to speak.   Then if the house is fairly close to completion, I will take them through it and let them imagine the finished product. If the house is not complete or is a state of shambles, we never take them thorough it. Most folks just do not have the imagination to make the leap from "Junker to jewel".

This is a situation that I am working on right now: We have two buyers in the process of waiting for houses to be finished.   In the meantime, they are working with one of our 3 mortgage brokers to make sure their loan gets processed, so they can be ready to close when the house is finished.   That of course is our best case. They have seen our other finished houses and are comfortable working with us.

I have said in the past that I do not negotiate with buyers, but the truth of the matter is that most of our buyers are usually folks who have been renting and they either see a house in progress or pick up a flyer and attend an open house. They will visit our web site which explains how they can ditch the rent checks and buy this lovely house. They aren't even working with realtors and they have not looked at a dozen houses like many of the typical buyers.

Last year I conducted a little survey and found that many of the folks buying houses in the mid-range only look at 3-4 houses before putting one under contract. That seemed crazy to me since I look at dozens of houses but that's the way it is. <u>Remember to never assume that the prospect thinks like you do about houses and your rehabbing business.</u> As far as our buyers are concerned, we are the only source in town for houses. If I don't have one ready today, I ask them to wait until one is ready. They almost never ask for a reduction in price. (I rarely give one anyway) and most times, I try and throw in a few bonus items, like a stainless appliance package instead of just white or black appliances. Recently I have been using only Stainless appliances.

As mentioned in the beginning of this chapter, we are only going to talk about the business side of rehabbing. Going to closings and how to structure your rehab sale is just as important. Let's talk about that next.

8. Seasoning and Title issues.

There is always a concern about "seasoning" on an investment house. "Seasoning" is the term used when referring to the title. Since we buy the house, it has to stay in the name of one owner for say a year or sometimes less or sometimes more. Each lender will have their own "seasoning requirements". That is part of your business to know which brokers will help your buyers get financed with whatever seasoning you may have on a given house.

There are several ways to circumvent some of these issues. One of the ways we use and my personal favorite is to take title to the house in the name of a trust. Particularly a land trust. I like to have the old owner put the property in a trust in the name of the family then I buy the beneficial interest in the trust. This is not treated like a title issue.   Also though I would love to go into depth about trusts and their benefits, we will have to leave that for another time.

The best trust courses are from William Bronchick and they work great for short sales and straight purchases as long as they are not REO, (bank owned,) the banks will not do a trust. I buy almost every house in a trust. The beneficiary is either my LLC or myself or my Self-directed IRA.   The buyers (and their lenders) only know about the trust.

I pay short term income taxes on yearly sales out of my LLC. (The IRA is a Roth so no taxes there). I've rarely had an issue with lenders or buyers when selling out of the LLC or the Trust. This is where using a title company who knows your business is helpful. I meet with the title company I'm going to use in advance to "educate" them on the trusts and the way I like to close.   I recommend you do the same.

Seasoning can be an issue.   Most of our buyers will qualify for an FHA mortgage and I do not conform to the recent FHA seasoning requirements.   That means we don't sell houses within 90 days when the profit is right and the buyer is right and the seasoning cannot be gotten around.   That also means we have to pay for a second appraisal if the house is owned by us for 91-180 days.

I work with mortgage brokers but my preference is to work with regular banks.   Brokers can be more expensive for the buyers and they have looser relationships with the ultimate underwriter/lender.   Less control.   I like to use the banks where the lender works every day with the underwriter. Each of them known and trusts the others.   Fewer surprises, fewer let downs.

Since you are rehabbing these houses, be prepared for the lender and even the appraiser to ask for the scope of work performed and occasionally receipts and invoices.   I resist giving that much information if at all possible but defiantly provide a scope of work.

Another way to eliminate the "sours of seasoning" is to use a lender that does not care if the house was bought in a state of disrepair and then renovated.   They can still do the loan and you do not have to care about the seasoning issue.   We have found that the larger lenders are difficult but any of the smaller banks and lenders is very flexible.   Even in these uncertain economic times.

Also, make sure you form an LLC or some type of Corporation for yourself and your business.   This way you can take the tax benefits from using the company instead of your individual name. You will avoid capital gains taxes and get the added benefits of all the great deductions a Corporation is afforded. Since this is only my opinion and in no way financial or accounting advise, Please consult a tax professional on tax issues, it is money well spent.

9. Buying and Selling Wholesale.

As a general rule, I do not care if someone else is making money on a house as long as I too can earn a profit.   The higher the price of the house, the higher the profit should be. Many say that a good rule of thumb is 65% of the ARV, (After Repair Value). This calculation does not fit my business model.

Let's say you brought me a deal with a house worth $100k and you put it under contract at$58 and want to flip it to me for $65, (a $7k assignment fee).   After looking at the property, I see it needs $20k In repairs.   The cost of acquisition, plus repairs, plus the most important cost, THE HOLDING COSTS for six months = no Profit to me. Now on the other hand, I have several "bird dog" investors who just go out and put properties under contract with the intention of flipping them for an assignment fee.   They bring me deals with houses that I can profit as much or more than if I went direct to the homeowner. Since I cannot be everywhere at once, this method is very useful. I even pay folks a fee if they email me a lead for a house they saw, that was sitting empty with the grass over grown.

I would prefer to buy from more wholesalers but almost never do. The market is very competitive and it's hard to find a truly good deal. Most wholesalers can get others to pay more than I will. New investors beware since most of these deals go to the new investor who invariably pays more. They overestimate the ARV and under estimate the repair costs. The end result is a smaller profit and sometimes, heaven forbid, a loss!

By not competing for the wholesale deals with "newbie's" I tend to make $5k-$10k per deal more on each sale. It is more work to dig out my own deals but worth it. I highly recommend you do the same. Each new deal can be rooted out through mail campaigns, yard signs, vehicle signs, business cards, web sites, email marketing and so many more strategies, it seems only logical to use everything in your arsenal to find as many of your own deals as you possible can.

Selling to wholesalers is a similarly short sided solution. I have sold many houses wholesale and will probably sell many, many more since it is a great way to move inventory when you need to free up your cash or when you have too many houses going at once. I use the assignment fee form which is available on the web site www.awesomerealestatestrategies.com You will find this is an easy form to use and the buyer simply closes and you get paid by the title company.

Tip: Don't get greedy when wholesaling a house and keep it simple. Put a small $5k-$10k assignment fee on top of the deal and be up front about it with your final buyer.   That way it will close and you will actually make money!

Always use an assignment fee form when re-selling your contract or assigning your contract.   That way no one will try and screw you out of your small fee.   I have had a couple of deals not pay me which Is totally my fault for trusting someone to pay when they did not have to.   If you have a form signed and it states "to be paid at closing", you will most likely get your money when it closes. That is the right way to do the deal.

10. Using Hard Money and Financing

When we first began investing in Real Estate, we've used our own cash reserves and home equity lines of credit and some amount of bank lending and credit lines on our personal residence. I was fortunate to have these resources so that I did not have to share a big chunk of my profits with a hard money lender. I have used hard money lenders and the gentleman I used most often was very fair with us and in his case I was happy to share in the wealth. Currently I am working on a new line of credit which is collateralized on several rental properties.

When you have to pay for your houses and rental properties, it hurts your available funding for additional rehabs. Since I want to step up my rehabbing and you may want to do the same, you can increase your LOC. (Line of Credit). Terms will usually be around 80% LTV and prime plus 2 points for my particular situation, you may have to pay more or you may get lucky and pay less. You can also consider the costs of appraisals and expenses since you will not be financing them.

Please do not go into this end of the investing business thinking it is easy just because you may know a lot about buildings. This business is tough. It's difficult to find Junkers that are priced right. It's tough dealing with contractors, realtors, sellers, and buyers. It's hard to find qualified buyers and seasoning will add a whole other dimension.

Often, new rehabbers take comfort in dealing with wholesalers who can give them guidance.   Like I said in the previous section, most wholesalers are not the most competent on keeping your objectives and best interest at heart.   Their numbers can often be "fuzzy" and please do not rely on their guidance. You may overpay and get burned without even knowing it until it's too late.

People come up to me and ask funny questions like "so, tell me how to *DO* the Real Estate business" or "so, how exactly do you work the Short Sale business?" It makes me smile since I do not have a one or two sentence answer. (I do however have a book they can take a look at.) You will work hard, you probably will make good money, and you will probably love it more than working for someone else.   I can say all of the things above are true in my life!

I speak with too many rehabbers who are in over their heads, disappointed and just want to unload their properties for what they have in them.   Most cannot even sell them.   Of course, I offer to do a short sale for them. (Smile).   More on that later in this book too.

On the positive side, it can be extremely profitable and I have gotten my start with the money made in rehabbing and for the most part, it is my true love within the Real Estate business. The best advice is to always check your numbers from multiple sources and forget your emotions...If that's possible, I still find myself falling for some mid-century modern houses, open lofts and old brick commercial buildings in particular.

On hard money; I prefer not to use it, plus I do not like paying someone points on top of closing costs. But if you don't have cash, you will need hard money and the best way is to shop around for the best rates and the person you like doing business with. When you start out, you will get 65%-70% LTV money and after a while you may get 75%-85% LTV. Expect to pay 12%-15% and sometime more. PAY WHATEVER YOU NEED TO PAY TO DO THE DEAL.   What is the alternative?   Not doing business at all! As long as you have the right values and can make money, pay the hard money guy, (or gal).

"You have to plan, project, and budget your way to success."
Shawn M. Tennefoss

Calculate your purchase costs, supplies, labor, holding and marketing for the <u>absolute worst case scenario over a six month period.</u> My personal goal is to have enough working capital to not need hard money altogether and still be able to rehab two or three a month.

Remember: Rehabbing is not for the timid.   It takes substantial investment in time and money.   If any book or course tells you that this is a part time job and only requires minimal time and money, they are pulling your leg. If you pay less, then you will trade for more time. You can have more time but then you have to pay someone to do the work.   I prefer to pay someone and be looking for the next deal or the next three deals!

"Forget about the fast lane. If you really want to fly, harness your power to your passion.   Honor your calling.   Everyone has one. Trust your heart, and success will come to you."   Oprah Winfrey

NOTES

Chapter Two

Short Sales

What is a short sale?

A short sale occurs when the net proceeds from the sale of a home are not enough to cover the sellers' mortgage obligations, liens and closing costs. These costs will usually include Realtors fees, property taxes, transfer taxes and title company fees. The seller is usually unwilling or unable to cover or make up the difference.

Most short sale sellers are either in default or headed to foreclosure, although this is not always the case and is by no means necessary to negotiate a short sale with the bank. A common misconception by home owners and Realtors is the fact that the house and homeowner/seller have to be in foreclosure or default to start a short sale. The new more lenient laws allow the sellers to simply be in a hardship situation, such as a change in income, loss of a job or increase in expenses. (Medical bills, taxes, insurance and living costs.).

Situations that cause a seller to be in this position include, buying at the top of the market, adjustable rate mortgage, loss of income, divorce, equity lines of credit, health and illness in the family, and high medical bills. Whatever the situation, even if the seller was just too greedy and tried to over finance and is now upside down, a short sale is a great option for *creating equity where there is no equity currently.*

Insider tip: Most folks are in denial and do not want to face up to the facts that the house will be taken in foreclosure until it is too late. It is very important to learn to handle homeowners with the utmost respect and privacy, so they will be willing to learn and listen to what you have to say.

In some situations the sellers have stocks, assets and high salary jobs. This can be a challenge with some lenders to negotiate a short sale.

It used to be common for the lender to want to have a promissory note signed or try for a deficiency judgment. Things have changed in the past year or so, and this is no longer the case. This is usually a good thing to find out during your negotiations with the lender. I try to request a full satisfaction for the mortgage with each short sale and most times I get it. Since 2004 we have helped over 250 families with short sales and have advised countless Realtors on how to effectively negotiate a short sale.

How do I know if a short sale is the right way to go with a possible property I want to purchase?

The first thing you will use to determine if a short sale is needed is usually a CMA or current market analysis also called a current value.

Let's use the value of $100k for easy numbers. If the CMA is showing me that the houses all around this one are selling for $120k, then I want to be selling at 15-20% below that to ensure a fast sale. Also include all closing costs and repairs.

Take a look at the example below:

Selling price:	$100,000.00
Closing costs:	$5,000.00
Repairs:	$5,000.00
Commissions:	$3,000.00
Profit 20% (at least)	$20,000.00
Offer to lender:	$66,000.00

This is a very simplified version of the "quick math" you can use to see if the deal has any margin left in it for you. Remember we are generating our profit from the lender not the sale of the house.   The house will sell for whatever it will sell for... but the lender can be negotiated with to take a reduced pay-off; a short sale.

Do you remember in the first chapter, I talked about (wrote about) making your money when you buy the house, not when you sell it.   A short sale is exactly the same.   We are going to get our equity, (profit) from the lender by negotiation the short sale low enough when we buy the house to have profit when we re-sell it.

Multiple lenders: If there is more than one mortgage or lien on the house, you will have to talk with all the lenders.   As a general rule, I use a 10% offer for any lender that is not in first position. Often times if you get the second lender to take 10% then you may not have to discount the first lender at all.   What many folks do not realize is that if the second lien is more than 30% of the current value of the house and you get it reduced to a 10% payoff of the total amount owed then you have just created a profit in the house without even negotiating a short sale on the first lender. This scenario usually works best when the homeowner is in foreclosure. The second lender will realize that they will get nothing if the first lender forecloses.

The presence of two or more lenders does make the short sale effort a bit more complicated but also more profitable. The second, third and sometimes even the fourth lender will absorb most of the loss.

Most investors agree that you need to let the actual lender know as soon as possible of the potential of a short sale, rather than the collection or customer service department, which is only interested in collecting a debt on the past due amount and not in working out a solution with the home owner. You may have to let the lender know you have an offer even before you actually do, so they can get the wheels moving and you can work out your price. This only works if you are the investor and not the homeowner or seller. We have provided forms you can use to help with the flow of the offer process on www.awesomerealestatestrategies.com

Within the bank you will need to contact the "loss mitigation department, which will be the group who will provide the list of documents, (although most are similar for each lender), they will decide if they want to work with you on a short sale and provide a person in charge of the file to negotiate with. Most lenders now want a Realtor involved and I have one that I work with.   I do all the work and negotiating but they use the license to list the property and as the agent.

The seller's submission packet usually includes the following: W-2 forms from the employer (or a letter explaining the seller is unemployed), bank statements for two months, two years tax returns, a financial statement and a hardship letter explaining how the homeowner got in this situation. I have found that the hardship letter is very powerful and I usually start with this document, immediately after the 3rd party authorization form. Since I am the investor in all of these short sale negotiations, I have the homeowner write the letter in a certain fashion.

The following pages have a sample of hardship letter, an offer example, Authorization to release information form as part of the financial hardship packet:

To whom it may concern,

For the last few months I have tried to sell my home with no success. No realtor can seem to sell my house. They tell me that because of the condition of my home and the amount of money it would cost to make the repairs that there is no way that they could find a buyer at a price that would allow me to pay off the loan. I have been laid off from work for many months now and my spouse has been ill and needing medical attention so the medical bills keep coming in and making it difficult to pay my house payments.

I may need to move out of the state and in with friends or relatives. I have accepted (YOUR NAME HERE) offer to purchase my home. Will you please accept that amount as payment in full for the money I owe on the loan? If not I may be forced to consider bankruptcy, which my attorney says I should file for. However, I am willing to wait for (YOUR NAME HERE) to help out the situation because I would like to get my financial life back on track in order to help support my family.

Countrywide Financial Corporation

February date, year

RE: **Loan #00000** Hardship Letter - Short Sale for address Wellington, FL 33414.

To whom it may concern:

I purchased my home t in Wellington, FL in 2006. At that time I was employed as a Realtor and business was very good. My salary and the possibility of a promotion and raise made me sure that I could easily support my mortgage. Unfortunately, a downturn in the market caused my salary to decrease to 1/3 of the earnings I was used to making.

Soon after I purchased the house my marriage was heading for a divorce after 19 years. I was having a hard time making ends meet so I had my son move in with me to help me with the payments and help me market the home. I tried to list it for $700,000 and I didn't get any response and then continually reduced it to $529,000 with no takers. I finally put the price to $520,000 and still I have not had any response. There are currently **154 houses for sale** just in my neighborhood! The taxes have also tripled in the area along with the insurance, which has made it impossible for me to make my payments.

I really love my house, but I know that I cannot afford it. I am single working as a Realtor with few benefits and no savings. My financial situation cannot sustain that high of a home mortgage. I want to sell the home, avoid foreclosure and salvage my credit. I know that a foreclosure on my record will affect me for years to come. I would ask that you please assist (YOURNAME HERE) of (YOUR COMPANY NAME HERE) in resolving this.

My attorney has advised me to file bankruptcy, but I prefer to avoid further destruction of my credit. I just want to move on and start over.

I deeply appreciate your help and understanding in this matter. If you have any questions, or need anything further from me, please contact (YOUR NAME AND PHONE NUMBER HERE) directly.

Sincerely,

AUTHORIZATION TO RELEASE INFORMATION

I/We hereby authorize you to release to _____or its agents and assigns any and all information that they may require for the transfer or payoff about my loan/account for the above referenced property. "Agents" shall include all real estate agents, attorneys and their assistants. You may reproduce this document to acquire reference from more than one source. Thank you for your assistance in this matter.

Lender:_____

Loan or Account Number:_____

Property Address: _____

The bank will also usually require a broker's price opinion or a BPO.   This is now a function that they do internally but it is most important for you to be the person who meets the broker at the house with very LOW comps in your hand to help with the valuation of the property.   We are not looking to "influence the BPO" nearly as much as giving them a way to "verify the value" of the offer you have submitted.   Make sure you have at least two repair estimates in your hand to give the appraiser to help with the price lowering.

Investors often ask me how long it takes to complete a short sale. Although the response times vary from lender to lender, it can take from two weeks to over 6 months to receive an approval of a short sale from the lender.   On average I would say they get done within 90 days for me since I have everything ready and complete for the lender.   This "streamlining" will ensure your short sale moves along the banks never ending pipeline.

When working in the short sale business it is critical that the buyers, the sellers, their agents (Realtors) understand and accept that the time frame is lengthy before they even sign the contract.

In addition, you will want to make sure you do not put yourself in a position that you have guaranteed 100% to the homeowner that you will get a short sale approved.   You should always have the homeowner sign a "CYA" letter that outlines each and every item of the short sale and explains in no uncertain terms that if you do not get a short sale, you will not buy this house. Each line needs to be initialed and signed at the bottom. It is recommended that you have your attorney use our template and draft something for yourself similar. The form is available at

www.awesomerealestatestrategies.com

Please keep in mind that a Purchase Contract is a legally binding agreement and once the earnest money has been deposited it is binding. It will need the necessary language within the contract stating that the lenders must approve the offer and release all liens on the property.

The seller or the buyer may face legal problems for failing to execute the contract if the short sale is not approved.

Many lenders ask sellers to sign a promissory note for all or part of the difference between the proceeds of the short sale and the debt obligations as a condition of the short sale approval. In such cases, the note gives the lenders the right to sue the seller and attach other assets if the note is not paid when due. Since this has put such a burden on the general public, the government has stepped in and insisted that lenders release the seller from the mortgage in full without any deficiency judgments. Hence, we are seeing most lenders now do not even try this tactic anymore. Just be aware it may come up and insist the lender release your seller in full. California has a non-recourse mortgage law already in place so it will not be an issue there.

Most lenders do not even send a 1099-c anymore but a few do send them. It shows the debt reduction as an income. Please inform the homeowner of this, but keep in mind, it is far easier to deal with that on the tax return than a foreclosure on a credit report. Having a short sale on a credit report will have adverse effects, inform the seller that they may want to rent an apartment in advance or take care of other credit needs before they get too far behind on their credit and the score goes too low. Most credit reports will suffer in the short run but I always tell my sellers that a foreclosure is the "kiss of death" where as a short is only a score reduction and usually re builds within a couple of years or less.

"All you need in life is ignorance and confidence, then success is sure!" Mark Twain

Where do I find leads as an investor?

One of the frequent concerns beginning investors have is where to find leads for short sale homeowners. I started going to the courthouse and buying the list of folks who have had foreclosure or lis pendis filed against them. Sent them a letter and asked if I could help. It was amazing how many folks just called me up and said they would work with me.   Always tell the seller you are an investor who will negotiate a short sale and buy their house for the purposes of re-selling it at a profit for you efforts. Most people understand you do not work for free and have specialized knowledge that allows you to help them.   The best thing you can do is help them avoid a foreclosure and move on with their lives. Sample intro letter below:

STOP Your Foreclosure Now!

Dear Homeowner,

You can **STOP** your **foreclosure** by selling your house for **cash** using a program that may create equity.

We will pay cash at a fair market value, not a distressed foreclosure price.   If you do nothing, hoping for a miracle, the law will sell your house at **Public Auction,** meaning your house could be sold for 25% to 50% below value.   Don't allow this to happen!!!

This is a money solution that will allow you to rebuild your future, but you must act now.   <u>**Time is your worst enemy: don't be embarrassed or humiliated by a lender who cares nothing about your situation**</u>.

We've been in a similar situation yet nobody lent a helping hand.   We want to provide you that helping hand by supplying **knowledge, cash, and our ability to keep your creditors from annoying you!**

What will we do when you call us toll free @ (YOUR NUMBER HERE)

1) (YOUR NAME HERE) will answer the phone personally and ask you several questions about your home to evaluate your homes' potential.

2) We can communicate with your lender. They will deal directly with us. We have the cash to handle past due payments.

Warmly,

P.S. If you want to reach me now call my cell @ (YOUR NUMBER HERE). All calls are kept strictly confidential.

"NO EQUITY??? NO PROBLEM!!!"

If you have a Realtor you work with ask for old listings to mail these, along with the list you get from the courthouse. Of course, all these lists are available online now, so no need to drive down there unless you just want to learn the process. (Always a good idea.)

If you see an abandoned house, you can do a "skip trace" on the owner and see if they are interested. Most folks who have moved out will be great candidates for you.

When I first started in the investment business, I had bought a house on contract to fix and live in but it gave me a taste of the profits that can happen.   So I started studying the first courses I saw written by Carlton Sheets (1).   Then the natural progression was to take it to the next steps which were another teacher named Ron LeGrande (2). He has an even more refined system to follow. This lead me to one of the most dynamic and motivational teachers I have ever listened to or worked with.

His name is Jeff Kaller (3).   They call him "Mr. Pre-foreclosure" and for a good reason! He works with his wife Sofia and let me tell you they have the highest rated following and one of the most dynamic programs I have had the privilege to learn. I NEVER RECOMMEND ANYONE OR "PLUG" ANYONE ELSES BUSINESS BUT I WOULD HIGHLY RECOMMEND HIS COURSES AND LEADERSHIP!!!

If I had to use just one system for short sales and just one personal coach and "guru" it would be him. Let me just give you a sampling of the ideas with their system:

(4) His course by far will give you the tools to locate, successfully negotiate, and acquire pre-foreclosure deals on a consistent basis. **Is it effective? Yes it is**! His Course is very informative, practical and down-to-earth simple. I am happy to have worked with him and Sofia and continue to do so to this day. I learned:

How to "flip" to a buyer for $25,000 profit in 45 days.

How to avoid the chain of title issues - legally! The words you say to a lender to generate massive discounts on properties.
Ways to make cash in on deals your competition won't touch. Building an empire with no liability. How to fund your deals with no out of pocket money! The system of generating steady monthly income while building long-term equity. Buying pre-foreclosures by going door to door. If that doesn't "wet your whistle" I don't know what will!   I did 22 deals with his system while living in New Orleans in the first year! (Before hurricane Katrina). I took that same success and duplicated it in Florida, Oregon, Colorado and Louisiana.

These guys want you to know they are buyers and investors. Use every method you can to get the phone to ring.

Tip: Make sure you have pre-printed post cards in your car and a note book or three ring binders ready to go in case you need to leave a message or write down any addresses.   This will ensure your success in finding and getting at least a few deals in your pipeline.   Happy hunting!

NOTES

NOTES

Chapter Three

Multi-Family

Buying apartments and multi-family units for the purposes of an investment has advantages. A wise investment will provide good returns and possibly years of income in this area of Real Estate.

Properties that have more than one living unit are considered "multi-family". A duplex or two family unit is the smallest type while the largest complex might have hundreds of apartment units. In New Orleans, we call these side by side duplexes, "doubles". Most are "shotgun doubles" which have each room connecting without a hallway.

Some of the many advantages of owning multifamily investment properties follow:

@ **Cash Flow:** Cash flow in multifamily is always greater than that of a single family simply because you have more rents under one roof coming in. The more units under one roof, the less risk you have.   If you have a single family house and you lose your tenant, you've lost 100% of your income.   In some instances, this could be your entire profit for the year.   If you had a three family or a triplex, and lost a tenant, you still have two coming in to pay for your expenses.

@ **Economies of Scale:** If you have six single family houses opposed to one six family building, you have six roofs to be replaced, six lawns to be maintained, six tenants to spread out through your city or town, etc. However, in your six-plex you have one roof, one lawn, one tenant base centrally located.   Economies of scale in your favor.

@ **Competition:** There is a whole lot less competition in multis than in single family.   The reason is simple. Everyone is teaching and doing single family "flipping". Many of the so called "gurus" make it sound so easy that everyone is trying it or doing it and bidding against each other on purchases. The smart investor will put multi-units in their portfolio along with single family houses. (I use single family houses to fix and flip to pay for more apartment buildings.)

- **Management:** Because of bigger cash flow and more revenue each month, you can afford to pay a management company or on site manager to manage your tenants and thus eliminate or minimize the hassles while you go out and do what you do best, (or should be doing best) find and finance apartment complexes.

- **Paydays:** Your pay days are a lot bigger when you finally sell your properties. This is because an apartment complex costs more than a single family home and because of this, they maintain a greater dollar amount of appreciation. For example a $100k house will, in a market appreciating 10%, be worth $110k while a three family worth $300k in the same market will increase to $330k. That's a full $20k more in your pocket.

We all know investors who have made a lot of money flipping single family houses, but if you think of the folks who you know who have become extremely wealthy and acquired lasting wealth, you'll realize that many of them did it owning multi-unit apartments. My personal goals include buying as many as I can get my hands on!

Apartments make money a number of ways.   Many beginning investors think that they only make money from the actual rent. There is a whole lot more to it than just the rent. See list below:

1. **Income** from the actual rents monthly or weekly.

2. **Appreciation.** The market can and usually does go up thus increasing the value of your investment without even doing anything. However, one of the great aspects of being an apartment building owner is the ability the owner has to increase value in a variety of different ways. If you compare this ability to other investments like stocks or bonds you can truly begin to realize why so many fortunes have been built by investing in multi-family properties.

    Forced Appreciation — Forced appreciation is any repair made on real estate that "forces" the value of the property to appreciate.

    Cosmetic Repairs: Making cosmetic repairs makes the property more appealing to potential tenants while also keeping current tenants happier. Repairs that can have a dramatic impact on appearance include painting exterior walls, painting interior walls, repairing the landscape around buildings and replacing aged, dirty and worn out appliances.

Raising Rent: This may seem like an obvious way to increase the value of an apartment building but it is truly surprising how many rental buildings are charging rent that is 10% to 20% below market rates. Many smaller apartment building owners manage the property themselves and thus find it easier to keep rents below market to retain tenants. This theory is flawed in practice because it doesn't take into consideration that, nowadays especially, many people will move from an apartment for reasons having nothing to do with the rent. For example, many people relocate for better job opportunities in another city.

Replacing Utility Equipment: If an apartment building owner is paying the electric bill for common area lighting he or she can save a lot of money every month by simply replacing all of the lighting fixtures with energy efficient bulbs. These all add to the appreciation of an apartment complex.

3. **Depreciation:** refers to two very different but related concepts: the decrease in value of assets and the allocation of the cost of assets to periods in which the assets are used.

The former affects values of businesses and entities. The latter affects net income. Generally the cost is allocated, as depreciation expense, among the periods in which the asset is expected to be used. Such expense is recognized by businesses for financial reporting and tax purposes. Several standard methods of computing depreciation expense may be used, including fixed percentage, straight line, and declining balance methods.

Depreciation expense generally begins when the asset is placed in service. Example: a depreciation expense of 100 per year for 5 years may be recognized for an asset costing 500. When a depreciable asset is sold, the business recognizes gain or loss based on net basis of the asset. This net basis is cost less depreciation. Depreciation calculations can become complex if done for each asset a business owns. Many systems therefore permit combining assets of a similar type acquired in the same year into a "pool." Depreciation is then computed for all assets in the pool as a single calculation.

Too many aspiring investors are out there spinning their wheels, wasting valuable time looking at potential investments that make no financial sense at all. Don't let this bother you if you have been one of these people. It often seems that whole real estate market is designed to sell you investments that are really not money making machines. This is due to a number of reasons such as realtors encouraging sellers to list their properties based on similar properties that have recently sold at inflated prices, private sellers who have an unrealistic idea of what their property is worth.

The reasons are not so important. What is important is due diligence. Finding the perfect apartment building that will make you money from the first day of ownership. Location is a factor that must be examined closely. It is much more interesting and complex than simply where the building is located geographically.

"Determining the value of an apartment building investment is one of the greatest difficulties that many new commercial real estate investors face." Ted Karsch (Commercial real estate investor)

Most people who invest in apartments have some experience investing in other types of real estate, typically residential homes or duplexes and triplexes. The issue that new investors face is the fact that apartment buildings are valued by different methods than residential real estate. In fact, it is usually quite easy to find the fair value of residential estate using a comparative sales approach. The comparative sales approach simply uses the existing sales prices of similar residential properties in that particular area and determines value based on an average sales price of comparable properties.

However, commercial real estate investors and appraisers use a variety of appraisal methods to determine the fair market value of an apartment building. These new methods should not deter the new investor because once they are understood they actually will help tremendously to locate the best apartment building for acquisition. Take the time to increase your vocabulary and learn as many apartment and commercial terms as you can.

Capitalization rate or CAP rate for short. As the new investor is searching for an apartment building his Realtor will supply him the CAP rate of the property. The CAP rate is a measure of the income produced by an apartment building divided by the cost of the building. For example: if an apartment building is purchased for the price of $1,000,000.00 and the property produced an annual net operating income of $100,000.00 the CAP rate of the property is 10%. (**Net operating income** is gross rents minus expenses.)

Net Operating Income:	$100,000.00
Purchase Price:	$1,000,000.00
CAP rate =	10%

An investor can also use the CAP rate to determine the maximum price he can pay for a property when he knows what the net operating income is.

For example, if the investor is looking at an apartment building that is seeing a net operating income of $150,000.00 and he wants to see a CAP rate of 11% he can determine the maximum purchase price as follows:

Net Operating Income:	$150,000.00
CAP Rate:	11%
Maximum purchase price:	$1,363.636.00

Insider Tip: This simple formula to devise the (CAP rate) of an apartment building is limited however. *The simple CAP rate assumes that the investor will be purchasing the property for cash and does not take into account the financing terms that will affect the investor's rate of return on the building. In other words the simple CAP rate is a good number to use when comparing apartment buildings as potential investments but more analysis is necessary to determine exactly what the rate of return will be on a particular building when using financing to purchase the property.*

The goal for the individual investor is to determine what the property is worth to him or her. The best way that I have found to determine the investment value of an apartment building is to use what I call the "Income Value Method" (IVM) to determine value which will tell you the maximum price that you can pay for your apartment building and still realize the rate of return that you are looking for.

The greatest advantage of this valuation formula is that it takes into consideration the terms of financing that the investor is using to purchase the property. Thankfully, this method is not that complicated and it merely requires that you know some financial information about the property and the terms of the financing that you will using.

Of course, a spreadsheet will help greatly in simplifying this formula.

Mortgage: Loan To Value of Mortgage X Mortgage Constant = _____

Property: Down Payment on Property (as a percentage)
                                        X Desired Rate of
Return = _____

Mortgage:	80% (.80) X 7.99% (.0799) = 0.06
+	
Equity:	20% (.20) X 11% (.11) = 0.02
Cap Rate:	0.08 = 8.0%

With this new "derived" CAP rate you can now determine your maximum purchase price for any apartment building and ensure that you will be realizing at least an 11% rate of return on your investment. For example, you are out looking at 14 unit apartment building with your realtor and he tells you that the net operating is $150,000.00.

You know that your bank will give you a 30 year loan at an interest rate of 7.99%. You know that you need to see at least an 11% return on your investment. You simply divide $150,000.00 by your derived CAP rate of 8% and you get the price of $1,875,000.00. You know that you can purchase the building with a 20% down payment and a 30 year loan at 7.99% and still realize a net return of 11% on your investment.

"There is only one success-to be able to spend your life in your own way". Christopher Morley

A quick review of the highlights of Multi-Family:

- ✪ Lower cost per unit than single family homes.
- ✪ Greater cash-on-cash return. Traditionally, apartment buildings offer a greater return than single family homes.
- ✪ Foreclosures! All of the families who have been displaced because of foreclosure are going to have to live somewhere! And most likely they will live in apartments.
- ✪ You start profiting instantly. You benefit from positive cash flows from day one. And you can live off that income, so you don't have to go to a job every day.
- ✪ You can afford a property manager. You can actually cut down your property management costs and headaches by hiring a company that specializes in apartment building management. Never talk to a tenant again
- ✪ It is easier to get seller financing. Apartment building owners are generally more financially astute and are more willing to help you finance the property. It is even possible to get 100% financing.
- ✪ Apartment buildings can appreciate faster than houses. Strong demand in metro areas with limited apartment vacancies can cause prices to soar.

☝ Pay HALF the taxes you now pay. Standard tax rates of 30-50% don't apply. You will be able to pay the capital gains rate of 15% by buying and holding.

This is not meant to scare you, but according to The Wall Street Journal, the average 35 year old person in the United States will need to have saved a nest egg of at least 3 million dollars by the time they retire at age 65. That may seem like an astounding number and it basically leaves investors few choices to build a nest egg of that magnitude.

The first choice would be to play the lottery and hope. I paly twice a week but it's not my retirement plan, just a fun way to dream a little bit bigger! Unfortunately, right now this is the plan that many millions of Americans are undertaking right now. You might be one of them.

The other, and more common route, is to contribute to your 401k and maximize on your employers matching contributions. This has worked for some people in the past but as good, high paying, professional careers become more scarce in the United States this route doesn't appear to be a wise choice for most people. Most people's 401ks are mostly invested in a basket of stocks, mutual funds and bonds. The problem with putting your nest egg into a 401k is the fact that you are basically counting on the fact that the stock market will be in a bull market when you are ready to retire. If not, you will end up like many people who in 2008, when the stock market nose dived, were forced postpone their retirement by another decade because the value of their retirement nest egg had dropped so dramatically.

So what is the answer to securing your retirement future? It just might be a strategic apartment building investment.

Here's why:

1) **Other People's Money**. As opposed to investments in stocks apartment buildings offer the opportunity to invest with other people's money. In fact, investing in apartment buildings allows you to purchase the building with up to 100% other people's money by using a combination of partnerships and traditional bank financing. In addition, the balance of the mortgage is paid off over the life of the loan using other people's money in the form of rent payments made by your tenants.

2) **Scarcity and Demand.** A record low number of multifamily units will be completed this year. The increase in rental housing demand is being met by a sharp reduction in the

supply of new apartments. Just to put this into perspective, over the 10-year period from 1998 through 2008, there's an average of about 240,000 new rental completions per year. Last year, there were 160,000. And this year, **completions are expected to be below 80,000 units, which would make it a 50-year low**. This level of new completions is actually less than the estimated annual loss due to obsolescence, meaning that **we're seeing essentially a net zero increase in the stock at a time of strong demand. New starts are not expected to approach historical levels until late next year**, 2012, which means it would likely not be until late '13 and into '14 that we'll see completions return to historical levels. And obviously it's the completions that are what's important in affecting the supply demand fundamentals.

3) **Demographics.** Roughly 3 million young adults had been living with family during the past five years, according to data from the Census and real-estate investment brokerage firm Marcus & Millichap, and housing experts estimate that they now generate about one-third of rental demand.

4) **Instant Returns.** Factoring in maintenance costs and other variables, an investment property should produce at least a 6% return on the initial cash investment in the first year after it is purchased. For example, an investor who puts down

$250,000 in cash on a $750,000 property would need to clear at least $15,000 in the first year.

What does all of this mean to you as an investor? It means that the time to begin buying apartment buildings is right now. I am not promising that you will be the next Donald Trump but I certainly believe that apartment building investing now offers one of the safest and securest ways to secure the comfortable retirement that you deserve.

The next step is to get started. But don't go out today and begin buying apartment buildings unless you are properly prepared. You need to arm yourself with all of the tools, information and market knowledge to ensure that you are investing in the right property that will not only continue to pay for itself over the years but also offer you a hefty monthly cash flow that will put money in your pocket.

Advantages and Disadvantages. Purchasing property for the purpose of an investment has advantages. A wise investment will provide good returns and possibly years of enjoyment in the business. Buying multi-family investment properties may have some disadvantages as well.

As we know, property that has more than one family living unit within the building is considered multi-family. A duplex or two family, (or double as they are called in New Orleans), is the smallest type while the largest complexes might have hundreds of units on a section of land in several buildings or dozens of buildings.

Some of the advantages of owning multifamily investments properties include:

- Multifamily units provide for the basic needs of people.
- People always need a place to rent, in any community for many reasons.
- Investor grows wealth over the long run.
- Simply by renting the units in several properties, the investor pay down or pays off his mortgage using the money from rents.
- A shortage of available dwelling units allows owners to be selective in their tenants and may include rent increases as the market allows.

Some of the disadvantages of owning multifamily investment properties include:

- Shortages of tenants due to changing markets send owners compounding problems. Investor can no longer be choosey with tenants.
- Vacancies are higher, lease rates decline.
- Management can be tedious due to tenant demands and market conditions.

Financing multifamily properties can be based on the income of properties themselves and the leasing or vacancy rates. These income properties support the debt incurred. The lender considers the property first and the investor second including the management company's strengths and weaknesses.

When buying a single family unit or vacant property the lender will look at the investors financial strength or credit worthiness first and the property value second.   Of course if it's vacant the value will be lower since the value of any given multifamily is based on the income it can produce.

The lender will evaluate the property according to its income from the renters. Any investor should provide an accurate income and expense report and projections that show an increase I the future. Software available for investors helps them create the cash flow projections, income and expense statements and vacancy projections quickly.

Leads. When searching for multifamily investment properties, think like a Realtor.   Realtors often send out post cards to certain areas in hopes of someone wanting to list their home with the Realtor. The investor can take the same approach and mail out post cards and letters to apartment owners by using a list purchased or rented from area list brokers or local government. Place a small ad in local newspapers.   Instead of simply saying you buy houses, think like a homeowner wanting to sell.   Do they need money? Probably.   Place your ad in the money to lend section.

Run several ads on Craigslist.org in the financial section and in the real estate section.

If you want to take a direct approach, which is what I prefer. You can search for properties that are in Foreclosure, Divorce or Probate. These properties are public knowledge.   I start by sending them a postcard, then follow up with a phone call or personal visit. These are properties that consist of four units or less.   Larger complexes are in corporations names. First, the phone calls which is a personal way to reach out and offer to buy them out. When you contact them in person, they may hang up the phone or shut the door on you.   This is normal since they are going through a rough time.   I always let the folks know that I got in this business by being in the same situation they are in. If I get them on the phone, I try to simply set a time to talk in person or a conference call for later. I let them know I am an investor and want the property for myself, not to make money on their hardship. I also let them know I move quickly so they can get on with their lives.

My Market. When considering the market in your area, take a look at what other multifamily properties are doing. What is the market doing? How is the property market in my specific area, my general area, my state? The market will help determine your return on your investment. A lower market will offer less of a return while a higher market will offer a higher return keeping in mind that expenses may change in each market, affecting your actual net income.

What you are looking for in any given market is the rate of decline or increase. I have purchased properties in a declining market and in an increasing market. You can make money on either as long as you have the appropriate strategy.

Property Value. An investor should consider the property value of the investment properties they are considering and the neighborhood they are located in. I avoid paying for a full appraisal until I have exhausted all the tools at my fingertips to establish vale. I use the internet, BPO's (Brokers Price Opinions) Comparable sales, rental prices in the immediate area, drive by's to look at other similar properties and I stop in to competing units to find out the specials, vacancy rates, etc. that they are dealing with.   It is imperative to consult a local property management company.   They are a great source of information about most of these items and may even know your prospective building.   If you are worried about telling them about your prospect have them sign a non-compete, non-circumvent agreement.

Profitability. The profitability of a multifamily property is highly dependent on the ability to generate income to meet the debt service and the other obligations to keep and maintain the property. You can still find good proprieties and turn them into profitable investments. What a tenant is willing to pay to occupy a given unit is the actual cornerstone of the investment itself.

Therefore it is crucial that investors understand local market trends for vacancies and rental rates when purchasing multifamily units. Rental market trends are fairly easy to recognize once you do a little research and maintain awareness. Watch a local newspaper, drive by or around rental communities noting how many vacancies they have and in which areas they are in. If you only see a few rent ads or signs or you surmise that rents are increasing, it is probably a signal of a rental shortage of units and a good sign for a favorable investment area for you.   On the other hand, if you see a lot of rental signs and rents dropping and too many "incentives" being offered, it could spell trouble for multifamily properties in that area.

The ideal situation is, of course, is when vacancy rates decrease .

Apartment property owners can be more selective about the type of tenant they rent to and establish a positive direction for the complex through the management company, perhaps even instigate a rent increase.   On the other hand, when tenants become scarce, owners might need to become less selective about the tenants and perhaps even lower rents or offer "incentives" themselves to fill the units.

Financing. Like any investment, it is critical that you establish a sound financing package.   You'll want to obtain a loan that doesn't place excessive burdens on the property, or yourself. Lenders evaluate multifamily real-estate based on income stream and the financial strength of the borrower and the property itself

When applying for a loan on a multifamily apartment, always present the lender with a clear and concise cash flow report and provide accurate income and operating expenses.   This will make it easier to obtain favorable financing.

Opportunities. Look for properties anytime you are driving somewhere.   I try and take a different route home whenever possible to explore different areas.   Go out of your comfort zone and keep an eye open for properties that may look slightly run down or lowered rents to keep the units filled.   IF these rental properties are in good areas of town or in an area that is improving, the current owner may not be aware of the increase in value or the upside potential. This would be a good candidate for a remodeling of the rundown apartment complex and can be quite a profitable venture.   Just make sure that you ascertain the costs of remodeling and understand what impact it will have on your income stream during and after remodeling is taking place.

Pure window dressings for the sake of appearances only, unless it has a positive effect on your cash flow or occupancy levels, are typically avoided by prudent real estate investors. Get a qualified contractor or even three, to give you a bid on everything you need worked on.   Whether it is a full remodel or minor improvements.   There can be hidden costs associated with your dream property. Otherwise, what you perceive to be surface issues can be in fact, a real con of worms that can eat away at any profits or cash flow you retain.

"Success in Business requires training, discipline and hard work. But if you're not frightened by these things, then opportunities are just as great today as they ever were."
David Rockefeller

Buying 2-4 Unit Properties. Investing in strictly 2-4 unit properties is worth considering, especially when you're just starting out, because it maximizes your cash flow and minimizes your expenses.

Multi-family investors know that rental income is almost always higher for multifamily investment properties than it is for single family rental houses. This can be critical for you to understand especially if you are just getting started in the rental business. Even with the down turn in the economy this has made most single family houses are too expensive to buy and rent out for a profit or investment purposes if you need a mortgage.

Further if you have enough cash to buy them outright then you shouldn't be buying single family homes anyway, you would want to look at larger complexes where your money can be leveraged against a loan and your cash on cash return is much higher. IN today's world, the single unit rent role is usually not enough to cover the mortgage needed to purchase the increasingly expensive since family house.

Multifamily investors enjoy reduced vacancy risk, because you're not simply relying on 1 revenue stream of income per property, you are using 2 or more income streams "per roof".   This means that if one unit is empty, you still have three making the mortgage payment, paying the taxes and expenses. However, in a single family if the unit is empty you have lost 100% of your income until you fill that unit with a new tenant.

If you want to start out small with investing in multifamily units, 2-4 unit properties have rent roles that are 2-3 times greater than single family homes. Additionally the vacancy impact is much lower.

Since we now know that our "per roof" cost is lower, it is important to understand that our "per unit" expenses are going to be lower and our income "per unit" is greater. For example, a single family house may cost you $180,000 in our area which means our "per unit" cost is $180,000, however a 3 units or tri-plex is $240,000 which gives us a "per unit" cost of $80,000.

Generally the cost per unit will go down the more units you have under one roof or on the same piece of property.

Another advantage of 2-4 units investing is you avoid commercial status. Any property with more than 4 units is considered commercial. This will lend itself to higher expenses in the form of interest rates, (usually 1-2% higher), larger down payment requirements, building insurance, rental property taxes, water and sewer, just to name a few.

The inspection scrutiny is lessened since commercial inspections are usually more stringent as the repairs and maintenance can be quite a bit higher.

Finding 2-4 unit properties. Some of the techniques we mentioned earlier will apply to smaller properties. Most multifamily investors make use of a rental property agent who will specialize in multifamily investing. Ideally your agent should have some of their own properties and have listings of several others for sale. If you want to buy multifamily properties you should be working with an agent who has vast knowledge in your area.

Most of the units we purchase are 50 years old or older. (make sure to do thorough inspections)

Be sure to use a strong and a thorough property valuation which will determine in part the rental value based on the number of bedroom in each unit.   So all else being equal, you'll want properties with several bedrooms in each unit. Not only do 2-3 bedroom units command higher rents but they also tend to be more stable.   One bedroom units often attract more of a transient population, which simply means greater turn over.

Following is a photo of my first row of "doubles" in New Orleans. They are side by side units. I bought two of the buildings then worked on each neighbor until I owned the whole row within a year!   We fixed up each one and rented them out once they were ready.   I worked with a local charity to find renters who were really in need of housing. They were full most of the time.

You'll note that each window is covered with plywood to prevent people from looking inside and to prevent unnecessary replacement of the copper and the fixtures, (because they get stolen sometimes).   As I mentioned earlier, you need to secure your re-hab projects.

These rentals worked as good income sources for over three years and were sold to buy other properties.

The main reasons for investing in multifamily properties are because they are the best and safest way to increase your monthly cash flow while increasing your net worth.

NOTES

Chapter Four

Note Buying

What is a Note vs. a Deed or Mortgage?

A Mortgage Note is a written document, which includes all the terms or conditions for payment and is a Borrower's promise to pay a Mortgage Note Seller or lender, such as a bank.

The types of terms and conditions included in a Mortgage Note are:

- Amount of the Loan

- Interest Rate

- Payment Amount

- Date of Payments

- Whom to Pay

- Number of Payments

- Balloon Amount if Applicable

- Payment Start and End Dates

Although a Mortgage Note may be recorded at the Courthouse, there is also a Deed, Mortgage or Land Contract also required. The Deed, Mortgage, or Land Contract is Security Instruments recorded at the Courthouse and serves as a Lien against the property. A lien states the property belongs to the Beneficiary (Note Holder) until all payments specified in the Note have been paid by the Borrower. Deeds normally also specify:

- Whom is responsible for Property Maintenance

- Whom is responsible for Property Taxes

- Whom is responsible for Fire and other Insurance on the property

- Whom the Trustee and Trustor are for the property

- Whom the Beneficiary is for the property

- Note amount

Therefore, both a Mortgage Note and a Deed work in conjunction together. One specifies terms of the contract for payment, while the other specifies who owns the property until the Mortgage Note is fully paid. A Mortgage Note that is not secured by a Deed, Mortgage or Land Contract would not be advantageous to a Seller since there is no rights for the Seller should the Borrower default on the property. One of the techniques I use is buying the note then foreclosing out any junior liens on the property. This can be very risky and is not for the timid.

Security Instruments. A Security Instrument is the official legal document which, when properly recorded, places a lien on the real estate property to secure the payment on a Note. The most common security instruments are Mortgages and Trust Deeds.

Types of Security Instruments

- Deed of Trust
- Trust Deed

- Mortgage
- Land Contract
- Contract for Deed

Produce the Note.

One of the defenses against foreclosure that is becoming more widespread is the so-called "produce the note" strategy. Numerous cases have been thrown out once the bank has been unable to provide the note to prove that it owns the loan. Without having possession of the original note and being able to produce it for the homeowners' inspection, a foreclosure may be declared invalid.

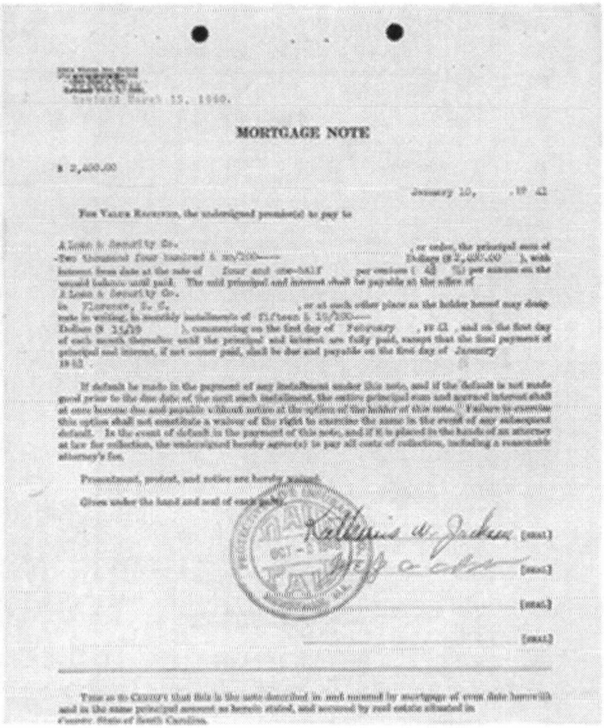

MORTGAGE NOTE

$ 2,400.00

January 10, . 19 42

For Value Received, the undersigned promise to pay to

[document text largely illegible/faded]

For homeowners to use this defense, however, it is important that you put together all of the information needed and do the required amount of research. Not every court will look kindly upon borrowers raising this defense if there is no legitimate basis for it. Homeowners defending themselves are already viewed as more of an annoyance than anything, so they should do their best to prepare for this type of defense.

The first question homeowners may want to ask is if a copy of the mortgage or note is already attached to the complaint. This can be a good starting point to determine if the bank has access to the original note, although a copy is not definitive proof of owning the note. Banks may attach a copy obtained from a previous owner of the loan but not have actual possession of the original.

Borrowers also may want to research if a copy of the mortgage or note is required in their state. Civil rules of court procedure would be the place to find this information, and can save homeowners a great deal of time if the state does not require the copy to be attached.

Also, homeowners should look in the foreclosure complaint for any affidavits from the lender relating to the original note. For instance, the mortgage company may include an affidavit stating that the copies of the note are true and accurate representations of the original. Another affidavit may state that the bank is in possession of the original note and mortgage. If these are present, the homeowners may wish to request that the original note be produced for their inspection.

Finally, homeowners should look into requesting the original mortgage and note to be included in the lawsuit paperwork for their inspection. This can usually be done through the discovery process, where homeowners are requesting other relevant documents and attempting to get straight answers out of the bank regarding the mortgage and foreclosure process. As other documents are requested (like payment histories), the original note can be requested to be produced.

If the bank fails to produce the original note for the homeowners' inspection, the case may be dismissed on this basis alone. Of course, borrowers should consult with competent legal counsel, but this new strategy to defend foreclosure is being used with more regularity due to the inability of banks to keep accurate records of the original note.

Steps to get you through this insane process include:

1. Contact your lender and inform them that you are not able to make the mortgage payments. Tell your story and provide the requested documentation. You do not have to continue calling them; they will call you. You have to know when to talk and when not to talk.

2. Start keeping records of every phone call: Date, time, phone number called, who you talked to and notes about who said what to whom. This may well be your strongest defense down the road. (I have 6 pages typed, single lines with my mortgage lender.) Keep everything in a binder in chronological order. This will help save your sanity also and it will be quite effective when a judge notes that the letters from your lender are unsigned do not have anyone's name (which is the case with Wells Fargo and probably others). It will also be worthy to note that contradictory letters will come from your lending

institution within days of each other. The lenders are shockingly sloppy.

3. Tell your friends and relatives. The more people know about your situation, the more chances you will have to get "lucky."

4. NEVER walk away from your home. The foreclosure process can be a short one or a long one, depending on your actions. You are in control, believe it or not.

5. Stop paying your credit cards. I hate saying this because in my own case, the credit card agencies were wonderful to work with, whereas the mortgage company has been a nightmare. However, your credit card debt is generally unsecured . . . except for your car . . . I lost mine to repossession. But the house is your first priority.

6. Do not pay for help. Call some of the counseling services just to see what they offer. Most counseling services, unfortunately, offer little. The largest groups that seem to get some positive results are NACA (NACA.org) and Acorn. I strongly recommend working with a professional group . . . one that does NOT request payment as nothing can be guaranteed. Also, It is now illegal in the State of California

to charge legal fees for services relating to loan modification

7. After the first three months the bank can initiate a legal action. They can send you collection letters. This is the time to request forbearance agreement. Sometimes it is free but usually your lender requests partial payments.

8. Do not rely on Home Affordable Programs out of Washington, D.C.. Sadly, it was not structured to help the homeowners. Trying this avenue is like hitting your head against wall.

9. An "option" is to request a short sale. I hate this "solution" as you do lose your home and while it does not hurt your credit as much as bankruptcy and/or foreclosure, it still hurts. I would go in this direction ONLY if there is no other choice.

10. How long you have until foreclosure is up to you and how much work you put into saving your home: It can be three months or it can be three years.

11. You may be your own best resource. There are ways to delay the process and stay in your home mortgage free while you save enough to move if you must . . . or figure

out a way to earn the money to get back on track, which is not easy, but it is possible.

THIS IS IN NO WAY LEGAL ADVICE, SIMPLY AN OPINION OF ONE WAY OF DOING SOMETHING IN A VIRTUAL OR HYPOTHETICAL SITUATION. PLEASE, PLEASE, PLEASE CONSULT YOUR OWN LEGAL COUNCIL AS NEEDED.

Buying the note <u>with the homeowners</u> on board. If you've been buying mortgage notes for a little while and are comfortable with the practice, you've noticed that there are a lot of pre-foreclosure homes out there with mortgages on them too. This is a large section of the mortgage note industry that remains untapped, but how can you get in on the profits with a defaulted property in the mix?

It is possible to buy the mortgage note on a defaulted property, especially with values over $1.5mil. When you use this method of real estate investment you still begin with the normal means of contacting the homeowner in pre-foreclosure through direct mail.

After you've spoken with the homeowner and they've agreed to sell to you, you'll have the homeowner under contract to sell their home to you. This is even though you are going to buy the note on their mortgage. You'll just have them sign the contract so they are locked in with you, and the homeowner doesn't turn around to try and sell the house to someone else while you are working with the bank. Once, you buy the note the contract becomes irrelevant.

How to Approach the Bank.

Contact the bank and ask them if they would consider a Short Sale to you. As previously discussed, you might try a short sale involving buying the actual real estate property at a reduced price and the bank writes off the remainder of the mortgage. Usually they'll say yes and begin to give you all kinds of information to turn in for final approval on a short sale. Then, you think,   'Hey, wouldn't it just be easier if I bought the note from you?'

If the bank knows how to do a note sale on a defaulted mortgage, then they'll usually jump on your note purchase because it is so much easier to sell the note than get the process of a short sale through their system.

Once You Buy the Mortgage Note

After some negotiation the bank agrees to give you a note purchase on this property and they accept your offer of say, $1,700,000 for their mortgage of $3,115,000.

By purchasing the note to the property you basically become the bank. You buy the right to collect the remaining $3,115,000 left on the defaulted mortgage. That's crazy, right? Nope.

Once you have the mortgage note you have a few options to move forward. You as the mortgage note owner could continue on with the foreclosure and kick the homeowners out of their home, not very nice since you did approach them first. Or you could get a 'Deed in Lieu of Foreclosure'.

The Deed in Lieu of Foreclosure basically means that the property owner gives you the deed to the property when they can't make payments on the mortgage. When you first approach the homeowners about helping them out of their property, you'll want to let them know that you aren't going to save their mortgage you're just trying to give them a clean escape from having that defaulted mortgage on their credit.

This means that you aren't going through with the foreclosure and the homeowner gets out without having a foreclosure mark on their record because they are just giving you the deed to the property.

The process of buying the mortgage note on a defaulted mortgage adds one more step to the basic process involved in a short sale. However, it's usually quicker, easier and lets you get your piece of real estate investment property sooner.

Buying a Note <u>Without the Owners</u> on Board. Since I specialize in buying high net worth notes, I thought it only fair to talk about the process most of the notes I buy get involved in. I normally screen for properties with a value of over $4mil in various areas around the nation that are going into default, foreclosure or are listed for sale as short sales.   When I look at these properties I use very stringent criteria for selecting which ones I want to pursue. Keeping in mind that the homeowner will not be involved in this note purchase.

Some of the selection criteria are use:

- The homeowner has to have vacated the property.
- The property has to be worth at least 75% of the balance owed on the property
- The loan balance has to be at least $3 million or more.
- The property cannot have any federal or tax liens on it. These types of liens could not be foreclosed or removed with title process.

When I negotiate with a lender to buy the note, I ask for the foreclosure process if any that the lender has already started to be assigned to me along with the note purchase. This is a very important and valuable step since the foreclosure can be a lengthy process and if you can use the steps already taken by the existing lender you have saved yourself a lot of work and time. Time = money, right!?!

"sub-performing" and "non-performing" loans.

Sub-performing loans
Often called a "high maintenance" account--that is an account that requires a tremendous amount collection effort in order to reason, cajole, harangue, and beseech the tardy borrowers to make their payments month in and month out.

In some cases there may be rolling late payments, back payments already added to the outstanding principal, or an existing forbearance agreement between the lender and the borrowers to stave off a foreclosure.

Non-performing loans
These are accounts where attempts to collect have been unsuccessful and the account is simply not paying at all. It is in arrears with back payments and other expenses due.

Often, lenders in need of cash liquidity are willing to steeply discount the amount they will accept for the sale of their sub-performing or non-performing loan accounts (the promissory notes). These problematic accounts are a drain for the lender both monetarily *and* from a human resources standpoint.

For astute real estate investors, opportunities can be created by acquiring these secured loans, which can then be "scrubbed" up and become performing again or simply foreclose and repossess the collateral securing the loan. Lenders sell these notes to create liquidity and get these loans off their books.

Ten simple steps involved in buying bank notes

The mechanics surrounding the purchase of ANY real estate secured debt instrument (the note) are essentially the same whether you are purchasing from a private note holder or from a bank-type lender.

Here are some steps to follow:

1. Verify the outstanding balance due on the note and the *actual* repayment terms of the note. I cannot stress enough that you MUST review the actual documents that were executed!

2. Verify with the seller of the note (the Assignor) the interest paid through date (or last paid date)

3. Verify the next payment due date.

4. Ascertain that the mortgage (or trust deed) is an insurable FIRST lien position loan (assuming you are buying a 1st lien). This is where a review of the existing mortgagee/lenders title insurance policy comes into play. Such a loan title insurance policy was probably issued when the loan was originated.

   You also want to establish the status of the property taxes, whether they are current or delinquent, and any impound escrow funds that might be held and be transferred to you for such payment as taxes and fire hazard insurance premiums.

5. Confirm the *value* of the collateral property that secures the note (that is today's fair market value). You can do your own evaluation, or have a BPO (broker price opinion) report done, or a formal drive-by, exterior only appraisal, etc.

6. Get the actual mortgage (or trust deed) security instrument assigned over to you or your entity. The assignment, once executed and recorded, will accomplish

this and transfer all rights, title, and interest in the instrument to you; the assignee.

7. Have the original promissory note instrument endorsed over to you or your entity (making sure the assignment of the security instrument and endorsement of the note match one another). The endorsement can take place right on the actual original promissory note instrument or via a separate note allonge (an attached endorsement).

8. Have physical possession of the original promissory note instrument given to you. This is the negotiable instrument you are purchasing and whose rights you will be able to enforce for non-payment of the debt.

9. You may want to obtain an estoppels affidavit from the Assignor. They will affirm for you the actual balance and terms of the note and might be useful in a later dispute with the debtor.

10. Obtain notification letters to both the note pay-or and fire hazard insurance agent notifying them of the transfer of the note account. (These are often referred to as so called "goodbye," "welcome," and change of loss payee letters).

It would be wise to further consult with your own attorney to make sure that what you are purchasing is what you bargained for. Once you own the actual debt instrument (the note) there are a number of options available for you to pursue in an attempt to collect or get the note instrument performing.

Buying Private Mortgage Notes. As we just learned, Mortgage notes are loans which are created when a home is sold. *Private mortgage notes* are funded by a home seller rather than a bank or lending institution. They are also known as cash flow notes, seller financed notes, and owner financed notes or seller carry-back notes.

Why Would a Private Mortgage Note be created?

There are many reasons a home owner might elect to fund the transaction privately. Private transactions can be approved and funded much more quickly than a bank funded loan. The lending criteria may not be as strict as they might be if a bank were involved, which increases the buyer pool for the seller's home. If the home is non-conforming, it may be difficult to impossible for a buyer to get approval for a mortgage from a bank.

What Happens when a Private Mortgage is funded?

When a private mortgage is funded, the mortgagee (the person buying the home) agrees to pay an agreed upon monthly payment to the mortgage note holder. The amount of the payment is determined by the terms of the loan, including the length of the loan and the interest rate.

Why Would an Investor Want to Purchase a Private Mortgage Note?

Private mortgage notes are usually sold at a discount. This means that the mortgage note buyer will pay a discounted rate for the loan to the current mortgage note holder and, in turn, will then receive all future payments made on the loan by the mortgagee. Privately held mortgage notes are sold at a discount because of the time value of money. This means that the value of the mortgage will decrease with time because of factors such as inflation. Think of it like this: If someone were to offer to give you either a $10 bill or a $20 bill, you would likely choose the $20 bill. But what if you could have the $10 today but had to wait 5 years to get the $20. Which would you choose now? Most of us would choose the $10 bill today because we realize that $10 today is worth more than the promise of $20 five years from now. This is the time value of money.

Why Would a Note Holder Want to Sell Their Mortgage Note?

There are many answers to this question. The note holder may need a large sum of money immediately for purchasing another home, buying a car, sending a child to college or to start a business. Whatever the reason a large lump sum of money may be more valuable to the note holder than smaller amounts received monthly. In addition, the note holder may not want to worry about whether the mortgagee might default on the loan or just may not want to deal with servicing the loan.

How Does a Mortgage Note Buyer know whether the Note is a Good Investment?

To determine the value of a mortgage note, the risk involved with the note must be evaluated. The higher the risk involved with the mortgage note, the larger the discount taken will be.

Consider the following criteria for evaluating the risk involved with the mortgage note:

- the credit worthiness of the mortgagee (the person making payments on the loan)
- the value of the property which serves as collateral for the loan
- the terms of the loan (interest rate, length of term, etc)
- the amount of the down payment made on the property
- the status of the loan (current, in default, late payments, etc)
- the loan to value ratio (the amount of money remaining to be paid on the loan balanced against the value of the property which serves as collateral for the mortgage note)

Individual mortgage note buyers will need to determine their own standards for assessing the amount of the discount offered on the mortgage note and the amount of risk they are willing to accept as in any investment. As always, consult your legal counsel for appropriate legal information in addition to this awesome guide! Even when a bank refuses to do a short sale a lot of banks have guidelines where they will sell you the note at a discount rather than the bank taking the risk of going through foreclosure. When the bank sells the note to you as a n investor at a discount the bank sell s the note at a loss and can write off (for tax purposes) the difference from what they were owed versus what you paid.

Once you own the note you can work out your own forbearance agreement with Jack. You can give Jack the time he needs to sell the property or Jack can give you a Deed-in-Lieu of foreclosure. He will just sign the deed to the house over to you (you are now acting as the bank). You can then sell the property on the open market at full retail or sell to a local investor.
Either way you make money by combining a couple of techniques together.

When you are evaluating a note for purchase and you are working with the bank you still want to pull the homeowner's credit report just so you understand all of their debts and the likelihood of any potential IRS problems attaching to the property before you complete your purchase.

We recently finished buying a note from a larger bank, (JP Morgan) which they had refused to do a short sale at anything less than $5.5mil but go figure I bought the note for $3mil! Since I did not have the $3mil needed to close on this note purchase, I simply sold the note to a final buyer or "principal" as we call them for the $3mil payable direct to Chase, and a fee payable to us as the transaction engineer. My fees usually range from 8% or higher I generally start at 10% of the note purchase amount.   This is not uncommon since included in the note purchase agreement are such **"value added" items as the foreclosure assignment** and title work that I have no problem with the premium and the buyer has no problem paying.   It is well worth their money and time.   It is like getting an investment package with a little bow on top, ready to open and they make money too.

However, buyers beware! Those looking to purchase non-performing notes **in multifamily** need to keep the following six issues in mind:

1. Make sure you know the foreclosure laws in the particular state in which the underlying asset is located. In some states, such as Georgia, with its non-judicial foreclosures, the foreclosure process is straightforward and can be completed rather quickly. However, in other states, such as Florida, the process can drag on for quite some time.
2. Find out what percentage of the multifamily asset is leased and, of such leases, what percentage of tenants are actually paying

their rent consistently. A high percentage of the property may be leased, but a high percentage of those tenants may also be behind on payments. What are you really getting for the money?

3. Know how to get your hands on the original note and all related amendments and assignments (i.e., allonge) thereof.

4. Try to procure as much information as possible from the lender about the asset before investing money on due-diligence investigations. The lenders have extensive files about each asset—you just have to push them to release the materials to you.

5. The condition of multifamily improvements is often more critical than other property types since the turnover of leases is so frequent (i.e., every year) and potential new residential tenants will simply look to another apartment complex if the property doesn't "look good."

6. If time allows, procure an updated property condition report before purchasing the note, but certainly obtain such a report before completing the foreclosure. The property condition report is crucial in determining any necessary capital improvements and that amount will be used ultimately to determine how aggressive a note buyer can be with the rental rates.

Photo of ocean front house that I helped facilitate the note purchase for $3 million with debt of about $5.8 million, (not a bad reduction).

NOTES

Chapter Five

REO's--Lender Direct

hat is an REO?

REO is an acronym for real estate owned and is industry jargon for foreclosure property repossessed by banks or lenders. If a lender or bank is the highest bidder at a foreclosure auction — or if no third party bids at the auction — or if the owner has deeded the property back, such as a deed in lieu — the property reverts back to the lender and becomes an REO. REOs are owned by banks. Lenders go to great lengths to sell REOs. For banks, however, bank-owned homes are a liability.

Where can I find REOs?

There are several ways to locate bank-owned REO properties. With the advent of the Internet, finding bank-owned REO properties is easy. Go directly to lenders themselves. Each lending institution, however, handles REO properties differently. Some lenders post bank-owned real estate lists on their websites.

Smaller local banks usually have one individual who is in charge of the bank's REO inventory. Larger regional and national lending institutions, on the other hand, have large departments that deal exclusively with selling bank-owned properties. Frequently, this department is referred to as the loss mitigation department. The job of the loss mitigation department is to mitigate the loss or minimize the damage caused by loans that have defaulted, which lenders call non-performing loans.

How can I buy a bank-owned REO?

Anyone can buy a bank-owned REO. The challenge for real estate investors is to reach the person who can make the decision to sell the bank-owned REO property. Each lending institution has different rules and requirements on how they sell bank-owned REO properties. Contact the lender and find out what they require to purchase an REO property. Ihave found that each lender is now requiring that the REO's to go through a licensed Realtor who will help them determine the market value of the house as close to retail as they can get. This is making it a bit more challenging.

Why should I buy a buy bank-owned REO?

One of the primary advantages of buying a bank-owned REO property is that investors are purchasing a property without liens or other encumbrances. Before lenders make REO properties available for sale, they typically expunge all liens or claims against the property. Any cloud on the title — a second or third mortgage, mechanics liens, taxes or any other liens attached by creditors — are wiped out. Moreover, skilled investors can negotiate with the lender's loss mitigation department to discount the price to a fraction of its market value. Besides negotiating price, many buyers of REO properties also negotiate favorable lending terms below existing market rates.

What are the advantages of buying bank-owned properties or REO homes?

For real estate investors and homebuyers, bank-owned properties and REOs offer opportunities that are not available in the pre-foreclosure and auction phase of the foreclosure process. Buying bank-owned real estate offers the foreclosure buyer many advantages:

- Bank-owned properties are usually sold at below-market prices with great terms like low down payments and low interest rates.

- Buying bank-owned properties involves less risk and less competition.

- Foreclosures that are owned by banks are usually clear of any liens that may have been recorded against the property.

- Since the seller of REO homes is also the lender, you can negotiate with the bank to have them pay for all or some of the closing costs.

- Bank-owned properties are usually vacant because the banks have evicted the previous owner, saving the investor or homebuyer time, money and emotional toll involved in the eviction process.

Buying a Bank-Owned REO Property.

Are you a real estate investor or homebuyer looking to purchase a bank-owned property? With the number of bank-owned foreclosures rising nationwide, there has never been a better time to purchase real estate owned by banks.

REO Buying Checklist:

- Inspect the Property
- Do a Title Search
- Negotiate Payments and Rates

- Evaluate the Offer
- Financing and Credit

Essentially, there are three different stages at which you can buy a foreclosure property. Investors and homebuyers can purchase a foreclosure property in the first phase of default — before a foreclosure auction takes place. Secondly, investors can purchase a property at the public foreclosure auction. And finally, a foreclosure property can be purchased from the bank or lending institution if no one bids at the public sale and the bank repossesses the property.

Once a property is repossessed by a bank or lender, the property will probably be listed for sale through a real estate agent. Good buys are available, but they require research, preparation, patience and persistence. Buying a bank-owned home in foreclosure isn't easy, and it's hardly without risk. Before you consider plunging into the foreclosure market, be sure to do some In-depth research.

Here is a list of things you can do to successfully purchase a bank-owned REO:

1. Inspect Property.

Most foreclosure properties are referred to by investors as "distressed" properties. Bank-owned foreclosure homes are usually sold "as is," which means that the 15 percent discount you just saved on the purchase price can easily be eaten up by unforeseen expenses — such as repairs not immediately apparent in an exterior inspection.

Many owners of homes that go into foreclosure have been struggling financially, which usually means that the house has not received needed repairs or general maintenance for a while. Some homeowners who lose their property to a lender frequently damage the property. So be prepared to do renovations and repairs. Hire a licensed home inspector to give you a written estimate of the cost to repair the property. Budget that number into your purchase price. Repair costs can be used later in your negotiation with the bank to reduce the asking price.

2. Title Search.

Once a home has been located, search the public records for liens and outstanding taxes. You can perform a preliminary check of title and then hire a title company to run a full, insured title search before closing the deal. Liens on the property can drive up the purchase price. Common liens typically are placed on a property for unpaid loans borrowed against the property, taxes or unpaid contractors (mechanics liens). These liens remain intact until the money is paid, which means that you may have to pay off the liens on the foreclosed property you are buying — even though you're not the one who didn't pay the property taxes. Banks should clear the title before selling but never assume this is the case — just as you would if you were buying a property from anyone else.

3. Negotiate.

Investors should be prepared to negotiate a lower down payment, a lower interest rate, a reduction in closing costs and a lower asking price. Many mortgage lenders may be willing to waive some closing costs, maybe even offer a break on the interest rate or the down payment. Moreover, some lenders might offer to finance the property at a below-market rate or with a lower-than-usual down payment. Don't be afraid to ask for a better price and favorable terms.

4. The Offer.

Although most banks want to unload their foreclosed properties, they won't necessarily do so cheaply. So you aren't guaranteed a fabulous price. But remember you're dealing with an eager seller. Even though the bank's REO manager or their listing agent might suggest that the list price is "firm," never be afraid to negotiate price — especially if the foreclosed bank-owned home needs repairs. When submitting a low offer, you need to substantiate the reduced price in writing and document your case. You should furnish photographs and cost estimates for repairs to support your offer amount.

5. Financing.

With good credit, many banks will loan the full price of the foreclosure or more. If the home is to be used as a rental, many banks will require only a 10 percent down payment. Foreclosure investors with a large amount of equity in another home may get a line of credit from their bank to purchase a foreclosure. When they convert the line of credit to a mortgage, no down payment may be required

6. Remodel/Repair

As we discussed in the first chapter of this book, re-habbing is a great way to make money. This chapter about REO purchasing just gives you an additional avenue to purchase houses at some type of a discount or "distressed" pricing. Anytime you can get a better value for the house you are buying the more profit you will have a t the end.

As I always say" you make your money when you buy, not when you sell". This is true of REO houses too. In fact, if you can find a lender willing to give you an even larger discount, you may want to consider buying pools of REO houses, or grouping together offers to allow for better discounts.

NOTES

NOTES

Chapter Six

Foreclosure

Foreclosure is a process that allows a lender to recover the amount owed on a defaulted loan by selling or taking ownership (repossession) of the property securing the loan. The foreclosure process begins when a borrower/owner defaults on loan payments and the lender files a public default notice. The foreclosure process can end one of four ways:

1. The borrower/owner pays off the default amount to reinstate the loan during a grace period known as pre-foreclosure.

2. The borrower/owner sells the property to a third party during pre-foreclosure, allowing the borrower/owner to pay off the loan and avoid having a foreclosure on his or her credit history.

3. A third party buys the property at a public auction at the end of the pre-foreclosure period.

4. The lender takes ownership of the property, usually with the intent to re-sell. The lender can take ownership through an agreement with the borrower/owner during pre-foreclosure or by buying back the property at the public auction. (Deed in lieu)

Foreclosure Buying Opportunities

The foreclosure process offers three bargain-buying opportunities.

1. Buying during pre-foreclosure (NOD, LIS-PENDIS)

2. Buying at public auction (NTS, NFS)

3. Buying bank-owned properties (REO, GOV)

Five Steps to Buying a Foreclosure (ACTUALLY A PRE-FORECLOSURE)

STEP 1. Find a Property

Buying a home in foreclosure can begin with you searching the internet and decide where you want to search for property. The internet allows you to search by county, city or zip code. We recommend starting with a broader search (Like County or city) and narrowing the search later if necessary.

Decide the status of foreclosure for which you want to search. You choose the status under Property Status on the Property Search page.

1. Select Pre-Foreclosure for Default Notices or Lis Pendens.

2. Select Auction for Trustee Sales or Sheriff's Sales.

3. Select Bank Owned or Government Owned for REOs (repossessions).

Property Details

The Property Details should always include the address of the property and the name of the owner, trustee or lender involved with the foreclosure, depending on the property status. Also included should be an estimate of the unpaid loan balance, which will appear either as the Balance, Opening Bid or First Loan Amount.

The Estimated Property Market Values is an important search and are based on comparable sales. Check Comparable Sales to view recently sold neighborhood properties and an analysis of property values in that neighborhood.

The date and purchase amount the last time the property changed ownership is also and important search parameter.

The Balance or Opening Bid provides a good estimate of the amount owed on the loan in foreclosure. The Default Amount (usually only relevant for Pre-Foreclosure properties) is the amount the owner/borrower Is behInd on payments.

STEP 2. Get Financing

Obtaining financing not only gives you an estimate of what you can afford, it also enables you to move quickly once you locate a property that interests you. When you approach a borrower/owner or a foreclosing lender about a property, secured financing will demonstrate that you are a serious buyer and are ready to buy quickly.

You can apply for financing with a financing partner.

STEP 3. Contact an Agent

If you're a first-time homebuyer and you've never purchased a home, let alone a foreclosure property, it is beneficial to contact a local real estate agent or mortgage broker who can guide you through the process of buying a foreclosure. If you work with an agent, make sure they know your priorities. Ask any potential agents if they have experience with foreclosures. Especially for first-time buyers, a good agent can be a comforting and helpful resource..

STEP 4. Contact Owner

Depending on the property status, the seller will be the owner in default, the trustee or the foreclosing lender. To determine the property status, look at the Foreclosure Status.

Buying a property in pre-foreclosure involves approaching the borrower/owner and offering to buy the property. The borrower/owner can walk away with something to show for any equity in the property and avoid a bad mark on his or her credit history. The buyer has time to research the title and condition of the property and can realize discounts of 20 percent to 40 percent below market value.

If the loan is not reinstated by the end of the pre-foreclosure period, potential buyers can bid on the property at a public auction. Buyers often are required to pay in cash at the auction and may not have much time to research the title and condition of the property beforehand; however, a public auction offers some of the best bargains and avoids the unpredictability of dealing directly with the borrower/owner.

If the lender or government agency takes ownership of the property, either through an agreement with the owner during pre-foreclosure or at the public auction, the lender usually sells the property to recover the unpaid loan amount. The lender typically clears the title for any buyer, but the potential bargain is often less than a pre foreclosure or auction property.

Contact Owner: Pre-Foreclosure

When a property is in pre-foreclosure (NOD, LIS), the owner still has a chance to stop the foreclosure process by paying off what is owed or by selling the property. The pre-foreclosure period can last several months, so you may need to be patient when trying to contact the owner in default.

The first step is to call the trustee or attorney listed on the Property Details page to confirm if the property is still in foreclosure. The trustee or attorney has the most up-to-date information if the owner has sold or reinstated the property. The trustee or attorney cannot answer other questions about the property.

If you haven't done it already, you'll want to evaluate the property's value and check for any additional loans or liens encumbering the property so that you can make an informed decision about whether the property is a wise investment.

If the trustee confirms the property is still in foreclosure, and you believe the property could be a wise investment, you should contact the owner in default as soon as possible. The quickest way to make contact with the owner is always the best, via phone, email or stopping by his or her address or residence.   Do not be scored of this approach.   I simply tell the folks right up front that "I am an investor who had the same issues and would like to buy hem out so they have no further marks on their credit report."

If the owner does not respond to a postcard you can try to send another postcard (the owner may have a change of heart as the end of the pre-foreclosure period approaches) or you can wait to see if the property is scheduled for auction and attend the auction.

One option is to call the owner if you can track down the phone number. Another option is to go to the property and try to contact the owner in person, as long as you recognize the ownership rights of the owner. We don't recommend either of these options if you don't have previous experience.

Contact Trustee: Auctions

Before the auction, you may have a chance to work out a last-minute deal with the owner in default. Usually a property is scheduled for auction just a few weeks before the auction occurs, so you may have to move quickly if you want to contact the owner.

Auctions can be postponed or canceled anytime, so no matter what the auction date listed, (even if it's in the past), it's always a good idea to contact the trustee or attorney to confirm. We recommend you call when you first locate the property and the day before the property is scheduled for auction. The trustee/attorney has the most up-to-date information if the auction has been canceled or postponed. The trustee/attorney cannot answer other questions about the property.

Some auction properties allow you to bid online for the property. If this is the case, you'll see a "Bid Now" button on the search results page and "Bid Now" links on the property details page. Just click on any of those to be taken to a bidding page where you can see more details about the bidding and submit a bid if you wish.

If you haven't done it already, you'll want to evaluate the property's value and check for any additional loans or liens encumbering the property so that you can make an informed decision about whether the property is a wise investment. If you believe the property could be a wise investment, you can attend the auction to bid on the property.

Most county websites usually have the auction date, time, location and opening bid. If any of this information is missing, you can often get it from the trustee or attorney. If you've never bought at auction before, we recommend you attend several auctions just to observe before you attend an auction to bid.

Contact Owner: Bank Owned

If the property is Bank Owned (REO), your first step is to contact the lender, whose information is usually on the internet. You should contact the lender directly and ask for their REO or asset management department to find out how you can view and possibly make an offer on the property. REO means "Real Estate Owned" by the lender. It's another way to say the property has gone through the foreclosure process and has now been repossessed by the foreclosing lender.

Some bank-owned properties will give you the option to contact the property's listing agent directly.

1. Contact an Agent to find a local real estate agent who can help you contact the lender and who can check if the property is already listed on the market with a real estate agent.

2. Other records may have more information, such as the lender name, address and phone number that was missing on the original property record.

3. You can contact the local property assessor to find out the owner's name and mailing address. Since the property is bank owned, the property assessor should have the bank or lender listed as the owner.

Contact Owner: Government Owned

Many government-owned properties are already listed with a real estate agent, Or you can try to contact the government agency listed directly. HUD and Fannie Mae have website for this exact purpose.

STEP 5. Make an Offer

If you have never purchased a foreclosure property before, we recommend that you have a real estate agent help you prepare and make an offer.

To get an estimate of the potential bargain for any property, you need to find out the estimated market value of the property, how much is owed on the property and if the owner has any other loans or liens encumbering the property.

Add together any outstanding loans and liens and estimated repair costs and subtract that total from the estimated market value of the property.

Based on your research of the potential bargain, you can make an offer. Usually the offer amount is somewhere below the market value but above the total outstanding liens and estimated repair costs. If the property is a pre-foreclosure or bank owned, you could prepare an offer similar to a typical purchase offer, contingent on a full inspection and title search.

If the property is selling at auction, you will need to make your offer, or bid, at the auction. In many states, bidders are required to pay in cash in the form of a cashier's check at the auction. You probably won't be able to conduct a full inspection and title search when you buy at an auction, so it's important to do careful research before attending an auction. Consult your local attorney before making any financial or legal decisions.

To help prepare you for what you might encounter in purchasing an REO;

1. Utilities Off:

Normally, banks don't pay for utilities once they've foreclosed on a home. If power, water and gas are going to be on, it will be at the behest of the listing agent. Let's say you have 120 foreclosed homes listed. Would you want to pay utilities on the lot? Not likely. Add to this the fact that if the water is turned off, people still consider the toilets a resource to be utilized. Right. Nasty. And if you want to view them after it gets dark, bring a flashlight. And a German Shepherd.

2. Trashed Carpets:

How do they do it? Trashed carpets are such a constant that I've concluded they have a secret website with a standardized recipe. It's gotta be something like the following:

· Allow 3 toddlers to walk around the house with red Kool-Aid. Spill frequently.

· Wait for rain, and then wipe all dirty footwear liberally on all carpets (even in the closets).

· Grind in the remnants of FCWT (Food Consumed Watching Television).

· Throw in some unsavory activity by Feefee (the un-housebroken doggy wonder).

· Let it sit for three months during a hot summer with all windows and doors tightly shut.

3. Bizarre Paint Schemes:

Maybe it's just me, but it seems that almost every REO I enter has a bizarre paint scheme. I'm guessing they hit up the "OOOOOPS" bin at their local Home Improvement megastore for the "SURPRISE!" factor. And no two rooms are painted the same color or painted well, for that matter.

4. Missing Things:

When people lose their home, they want to get back at "The Man." So they take stuff. They figure, "If I'm gonna lose; I'm not going down without some souvenirs." To make things even worse, once a home appears to be vacant for any length of time, it magically materializes on opportunists' radar. I'm convinced they've got a secret organization out there somewhere. They swoop in and "avail themselves" to various items. The following are the sorts of things I've seen "missing-in-action":

· Heaters and air conditioning units

· Kitchen cabinets and counters

· Closet units

· Any appliance that can be removed in any fashion

· Toilets

· Bathroom sinks and vanities

· Light fixtures (including recessed can lights)

· Doors (including the front door)

· Windows

· Copper pipes and wiring

5. Unpermitted Renovations:

Where do I begin? Here are a few standards:

· Garage conversions

· Extra bathroom in the garage

· Dubious kitchen and bath "remodels"

· Extensions to the rear of the home

6. Unlawful Residents:

There are a few options in this category. Four-legged critters include the rodent varieties found in your locale, including rats. There are also some in the two-legged variety that may include the following:

- Vagrants who broke in and now call this "their" digs. Shopping carts in the vicinity give this one away fairly quickly.

- Renters who were rented the home under false pretenses by scam artists who, (1) ran a Craigslist ad, (2) showed up to collect first and last month's rent and (3) handed the new "tenants" the keys. It's a common scam in some areas.

-

7. Owner Induced Contusions and/or Vandalism :

Run into a hard southbound object while moving in a northerly direction and you will end up with a bruise, black eye, bump, etc. Can be nasty. Whether it's kids trashing stuff "for fun" or a family member takin' out their rage, the result is the same. If you are a house and you encounter hard, moving objects, contusions look like the following:

- Holes in walls (often surrounded by shoe prints)
- Holes in doors (ditto)
- Bashed in corners (from moving furniture in a "non-professional mover" manner)
- Broken windows
- Broken mirrors (bathroom and mirrored closet doors)

8. Mold and Mildew:

Any home left shut up for long periods of time without ventilation can experience mold and mildew, especially in damp climates or seasons. Add to this the occasional person who, in total distain for future occupants, "leaves his mark" before he leaves and it can get pretty nasty.

Don't be discouraged – the idea here is to let you know what you might encounter so you'll be prepared. Some REOs are actually quite nice. Unfortunately, there are others that are, well... not so much. Do your homework, order inspections, consult contractors for estimates and you may very well end up with ...
A NICE HOME!

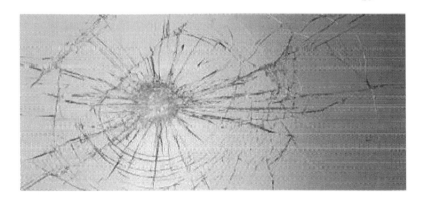

I've learned a few things along the way. No matter what anyone says, the process is WAY different than buying a home through a "normal" sale. I'm constantly bombarded with buyer questions about REOs (foreclosed bank owned properties), so I'll try to answer the most common questions here.

1. How do I locate an REO?

Finding an REO is as easy as asking your Realtor to send you a list of local foreclosed homes. Kind of. Most banks post their entire inventory on the local MLS, making it very easy for your Realtor to pull a comprehensive list and sift out the short sales.

There's one issue, however, that you need to understand. In areas such as the San Francisco Bay Area, there are many local MLSs. Many of these currently do not share information with each other. As an example: if a listing agent based in San Jose (MLSListings MLS) gets an REO listing in Fremont, they may or may not post it on the MLS that services Fremont (BayEast MLS). They be might not want to pay the MLS fees for the Alameda County MLS and will simply post it in the Santa Clara County MLS instead. Strange, but true. Any search of the BayEast MLS is therefore not going to pull up Fremont listings posted in San Jose. Thinking that's kinda dumb? Me too.

Anyway, since ALL local MLSs post to sites such as Trulia.com and Realtor.com, a quick search of sites such as these will locate any additional properties that won't show up in a local search. Be aware, however, that many short sales will also show up, and may not be identified as such. That's how your Realtor gets grey hair ...

2. Can I get an REO at an auction?

Yes, however ... in this area, the REOs that make it to auction are the ones that didn't sell while on the MLS. We are talking used, abused, neglected and seriously distressed properties. Bring your contractor ... and a big dog.

3. What can I expect to see when I view an REO?

Anything under the sun!! Read the previous section please. Conditions in REOs vary as much as the surface conditions of the planets in orbit around our sun ...

4. What will the bank do to fix up and/or repair the property?

How about ... nothing. Nada. Zip. Zilcho. Did I mention Niente, Rien and Nichts? Once it is on the market, what you see is what you get. You will be buying the property "AS-IS" with no exceptions. Broken windows? Trashed carpets? Holes in the walls? It's on you. Section 1 clearance? You again. And here is where it gets a bit tricky. If you are planning on using an FHA loan to purchase the home, you need to make sure it is habitable before you write an offer. The FHA will not provide a loan for a property they categorize as uninhabitable or having substantive issues. If they discover Section 1 issues, leaky roofs, inoperative mechanical systems or other visible issues, they will want these items repaired PRIOR to closing. And that means by you, since the bank will not make any repairs. Y-O-U. Personal opinion: spending money to make repairs on a home you do not yet own is VERY risky and I don't recommend it at all.

5. What about any existing liens against the property? What happens to them?

Banks will convey a clean title to you when you purchase the home. They have to – no lender will fund a loan on a property that has a clouded title. Existing mortgages, property taxes, outstanding HOA fees, IRS liens, mechanic's liens – all will be cleared from the title before your purchase. You will start paying all the normal fees (taxes, HOA, etc.) from the actual day your transaction closes.

6. What about appliances or other personal property in the home?

If you see even a small number of REOs, you will begin to see a theme. Missing things. As in, the previous owners took some souvenirs with them as they departed. Some mementoes by which to remember their old digs. Like the fridge, dishwasher, washer and dryer and … the range. Think the nice bank will replace those for you? See #4 above. Lucky enough to pick a home with some of those things there? Don't count on them being there when it closes … they may be and they may not be. Absolutely no guarantee. Reason is this: believe it or not, most appliances, since they are readily removable, are considered personal property. Banks cannot convey personal property.

Appliances there when you carry your bride over the threshold? Wonderful! You win! Not there? Sorry

7. What do I need to provide to write an offer on an REO?

You will need to plan to submit the following items with offers – have these entire ready BEFORE you start looking for a home:

· **Pre-Approval Letter:** must be on a lender's letterhead (don't even try with a Prequalification letter).

· **FICO Scores**: can be obtained from your lender (first two pages of the credit report will do).

· **Verification of Funds**: what % are you putting down? You'll need verification that you actually already have the funds. Provide photocopies of the accounts where the down payment money is currently on deposit. Getting a gift? Have an official gift letter in hand. Make sure you understand the gift rules – ask your lender.

· **Deposit Check**: for 1% of the purchase price (Good Faith Deposit) made out to "Title Company".

8. Are the banks looking for anything special in an offer?

Banks are like water and electricity – they flow down the path of least resistance. They absolutely DON'T like FHA loans and will go out of their way to avoid dealing with someone who has one. Sorry … it's true. They love a minimum of 10% down and conforming loans. If two offers come in at the same price – a conforming and an FHA deal – they will take the conforming offer EVERY TIME.

9. Can I ask for help with closing costs?

Yes! Banks often provide help with closing costs. However, make sure that you understand that in a multiple offer situation, your net price to the seller must match other competing offer's net prices.

10. What does my Realtor need to know to write an offer?

Hopefully, you'll be using a Realtor that has a lot of experience getting REO offers accepted by banks. However, just in case that's not so, I've written a post that will help your Realtor write offers that banks and their asset management companies want to see.

11. I understand that the bank will issue an Addendum or Counter Proposal to my offer. What can I expect?

Bottom line: <u>the bank will remove anything in your favor and substitute language in their favor</u>. Such as:

· They may ask for an **increased deposit**.

· They may try to **shorten the close of escrow** to 21 days. *Don't let them.* They will include **per diem charges** that you will incur should you not close escrow on the agreed upon date. These "fines" can be as high as $150.00 a day. If it's the fault of you or your lender that escrow closes late, you'll pay. It it's the bank's fault, you'll still pay. Don't think it's fair? Bummer. The bank has already taken a bath on the property: they want to make their pain go away by sharing some of the pain with you. It's called an incentive to close on time.

· They may change your **contingency time periods**. Typical periods are 7-10 days for Inspections and 10-12 days for your loan and appraisal. They may even change your contingency removals from active to passive. MAKE SURE YOU AND YOUR AGENT KNOW THIS.
· They may counter out any **requests for them to cover fees** such as title and escrow, home warranties, County and City transfer taxes, HOA fees and so on.
· They will counter out any requests for **personal property**.
· They might counter out any **liquidated damages** or **arbitration language**.

· **DON'T EVEN THINK ABOUT ASKING FOR REPAIRS**. Their documents will contain "AS-IS" language.
· (Sometimes, if there were **tenants** that were evicted who did not get their good faith deposit returned to them, the bank will make sure you know it is YOUR responsibility to deal with them.)

12. What kind of a price break can I expect to get because it's an REO?

First of all, the days of lowball offers on REOs are dead. Most likely folks making extremely low ball offers to banks wind up with no house. It was fun while it lasted, now get over it. Secondly, REO listing agents have learned to price their listings VERY competitively and, if it's a nice property in decent condition and in a good location, expect multiple offers. However, if it's been on the market over 60 days, all bets are off. Give it your best shot!

13. Will the REO listing agent communicate effectively with my agent to discuss terms, any current offers, suggested offering price, etc.?

The listing agents for REOs are without exception the most frustrating group of people to deal with I've ever encountered in my entire life. They do not communicate, will not tell your agent how many offers are currently in, will not give any information concerning prices of existing offers ... will not even answer their phones in MOST cases. They prefer communication by email only and like one word answers. I could go on and on here ... but I'll save my diatribe for a group that actually cares.

Bottom line: in most cases you'll need to write your offer totally blind.

Count on writing at the maximum price at which you are comfortable, throwing it into the mix and seeing if emerges a winner on the other end. And count on a few frustrations in the process:

· The listing agent may not actually verify to your agent that the offer has been received.
· The bank may take up to a week to respond to the offers.
· You may or MAY NOT get a response back from the listing agent that the offer has been rejected. When the MLS goes pending and your agent has not yet received a call or email, that's a clue. That you didn't get it. Strange but true.

14. Once my offer has been accepted, will the process go smoothly and quickly?
Maybe. The bank may get the signed and ratified documents back to you within a day or so. If you're lucky. Or not. We've had them take up to 10 days.
That's a whole week and a half before we can submit the docs to your bank to get things going on your loan. Need additional documents signed by the bank in the middle of the transaction? Count on more waits. And meantime, the per diem time clock is ticking away.

15. What kind of disclosures can I expect to receive?

None. The banks cannot and will not disclose anything. They never lived there and have more than likely never seen the property in question. In fact, you know more than they do! They will fill out the mandatory state required disclosures, but they will not contain any information that will be helpful to you in any way. It is up to you to thoroughly investigate the property. I've even had the REO listing agent ask ME to provide the disclosures.

16. What kind of reports can I expect to get from the bank?

The bank WILL NOT purchase any inspections of any kind. We recommend that you, as the buyer, thoroughly inspect the property on your own dime. You can only expect to get the following reports from the seller:

· Natural and Environmental Hazards report

· Preliminary Title Report

· Any inspection reports that have surfaced from an earlier transaction.

17. Can I choose my own title company?

No. It won't happen – banks do hundreds of transactions and they want to talk to the same people for all their transactions. Makes sense for them. Don't like it? Don't write an offer. Think it might be a RESPA violation? Get over it.

However, you CAN ask for the bank to cover title and escrow fees. They just might do it. Then again, they might not. And you need to know that a Northern Florida transaction may end with a closing company in Miami and a Title Company in northern Florida somewhere not even close to you. Don't let it confuse you, just allow for the entire day to close some of these transactions, or have your assistant go to the closings if you're on another project.

When I bought my first REO, I thought that it would be impossible to pay for more than one and never dreamed we could do one per month! However, once I started talking to private investors about the "system" I had developed and offered them great returns to invest with us, while securing them with the actual real estate; folks were more than willing to lend us money. Don't sell yourself short when it comes to how important this knowledge and your expertise will be, you too can invest wisely and make money on REO's if you apply the same common sense principals we learned here.

"Make your money when you buy, not when you sell"!

NOTES

NOTES

* * *

Chapter Seven

Raising Private Capital

There are numerous ways to put together a "no money down" real estate deal. They all revolve around the same principle which is to utilize someone else's capital, whether that source is the bank, the end buyer, or a private investor. "No money down" can be a misleading term. Instead, it really should be called "using other people's money real estate investing". You know, OPM, (other people's money)! Having said that, one of the most common ways to get a deal done is to use an end buyer's capital. However, there are laws in place now that can prevent a closing from taking place using your end buyers

money. There are transactional monies you can use and you can pay for a double closing which is recorded and taxed but we have discussed that previously in the "seasoning section". Unfortunately, most investors find it tough to raise private capital.

So why do many investors struggle with raising capital?

I've been to dozens of real estate investment clubs. Generally, the two most common things you'll see investors ask for is a. investor contracts and b. to take a look at their deal. In the case of b, ask them about their deal, they give you some sort of vague description. "It's a great deal on the East side, only XX dollars." The problem is that it doesn't convey the necessary information and it's vague and untargeted. Good marketing plans are never vague and untargeted.

Compare that to a professional real estate investor

There are a lot of good and bad real estate agents alike but one of the reasons they become a real estate agent and join a brokerage is because of the marketing system that it provides. When you walk into a home that is listed with an agent, they hand you an MLS listing that summarizes the home, business cards, and often additional pamphlets or brochures. They are treating their real estate business like a business and so should you.

Every investor that I know who is successful in raising large amounts of capital, whether it be private capital funds, large numbers of lease-option tenants, short sale and wholesale end buyers, or private lenders all have top notch due diligence packages. If you want to have access to these same resources, you need a top notch due diligence package as well. If you do the thinking for the end investor and make your due diligence package pretty, your conversions will go through the roof. If you go the investment club and try and persuade your local investor with nothing in hand, you'll be like most newbie's that don't close deals. Do the work ahead of time. You don't even need to be a designer as you can outsource that work on freelancer.com, elance.com, or craigslist.com for a very low cost.

A few things your due diligence report should contain

These aren't the only things a good real estate investment report should contain but it's a good starting point.

- *Comparable sales*

You can illustrate what a solid deal your investment actually is by showing your investors how much your property is already under market value. You should probably also highlight the difference between your asking price and the market comparable by utilizing something like "instant equity" and drawing attention to that on your purchase.

- *Pictures*

People are visual people and real estate is a tangible item. The more pictures you can include with your package the better. It will help your end investors quickly size up the area and home condition.

- *Features and Benefits of the Property*

You should look at the listings for the top realtors in your area and model some of the home features and benefits they bring attention to in their listings. Very often you'll find that average realtors have boring MLS listings and often the top agents have very detailed information on their listing. Make that investment package come to life.

@ How to sell my end money source?

The good news is that you really don't have to. Most end buyers, investors, or private capital sources will have their own criteria for investments and real estate. If you try and force them to invest outside their comfort zone with something that doesn't match their criteria, they just won't usually do it. They didn't usually acquire their money by accident and so these are generally knowledgeable people especially in regards to their own real estate investment criteria. By doing all the presentation work ahead of time, you're not selling them on the investment. Rather, you're selling them on your competence level and knowing what how to spot a solid deal. By showing this in the most visually impactful way possible, your money source will take you much, much more seriously.

So if you want to close deals, you have to make an investment package that makes it a no brainer for your money source. Marketing is your business!

@ **Here are some ideas to get you started.**

1) Create a target list of associations and places where wealthy folks would likely go?

- Business Groups
- Social Groups
- Wine tastings
- Wealthy people organizations
- Charitable Organizations
- Gallery openings
- High-end realtors

2) Decide how you want to market to them.

- Direct Mail or Post cards.

- Personal contact.

- Utilizing the Self directed IRA.

- List Broker.

3) Develop a perfect Introduction.

- Who you are:

- Why you are alike. Business in the area, real estate interests, etc.

- What it is that you do? Sound intriguing. Emerging markets around the Nation.

- How you do what you do? <u>I pay higher than conventional returns.</u>

<u>AND I ACCEPT PARTNERS!</u>

4) Prepare your conversation.

You will usually get two big objections and if you can learn to overcome these, you will be on the path to success in using private money.

The two big questions:

- ➢ Have you ever done a deal before? Or in other words, how experienced are you with other people's money?

➢ How much "skin" do you have in the game? Or How much of your own money do you have invested?

The two big answers:

➢ Be honest.   "I have participated in several deals with my investor group" or "I have over 9 years experience buying and selling Real estate and this is the next step in the culminated process".

➢ " I have my reputation at stake, number one" or " The equity that I bring to the table is my experience, the scouting of the deals and the ongoing management"

5) Put together a *Persuasion Package.*   The use of a 3 ring binder may be old school but works great to just flip through your information.   I now use an I Pad and simply "flick" to the pages I want to show them.

You can use a laptop as long as it doesn't seem like a big production since the potential investor will lose interest and feel uncomfortable with a bunch of cords, set up time, etc. Below are some of the things I like to include in my "show me packet". I will go over each in detail:

☝ Deals I've completed or participated in with other partners.

- ☝ Real Estate Education, Awards, Memberships and Associations.
- ☝ Life accomplishments.
- ☝ Buyers and Sellers Testimonials.
- ☝ People who say "good things" about you or your business.
- ☝ Items you may have in common.

Build Trust and Rapport with your Packet.

Tip: *You will close about 25% more conversions or prospects if you use something visual. Always include a photo or two of your family.   Everyone has some type of family—something in common!*

A Laptop, a three ring binder, an I Pad or any other form of presentation binder you want to use is great, just get out and talk with people.

--- **Give back as soon as possible**---Then talk with folks about that too!

"The (your name here) group gives back to the community by creating quality housing and by providing for the community's needs through special projects.   This is accomplished by ensuring our investors receive a secure return on their money through their investment in Real Estate" Anything similar will work and REALLY GIVE BACK whenever possible, you'll see it come back to you with dividends.

NOTES

NOTES

Chapter Eight

Income is not Freedom

Actively working for income is not going to make me financially secure because that income can suddenly be gone if I stop working, or worst yet, if I'm fired. I had an office job, I've actually had several. I've worked as an auto mechanic, a lumber broker, a salesman, a marketing director, and a few other "positions". They all seemed like great jobs at the time. These were good jobs and decent money; however, it took me until the last few years to realize what a silly system I was living. You have the opportunity to use this book as a "short cut" to avoid some of the same pit falls I've made and give yourself the upper hand when it comes to really being FREE!

So what does it mean to be "free"? It seems that it means different things to different people. I'd like you to start this chapter by asking yourself what "freedom" means to you? It may be that just working from home on a lifelong dream is what it means for you or maybe having enough income to get on your bike and ride for two hours every morning, then spend the rest of the day with the one you love. Perhaps it's travelling the world and enjoying all the things this beautiful planet has to offer.

I can tell you that all the things above are what it means to me. My wife and I have had the privilege to work for ourselves, travel the world, and travel the USA, Canada and Mexico. Below are a few of the "dream projects" we wanted to accomplish and have. We did this by converting the money we made into income that showed up at our door whether we showed up or not!

We started with a single house, spent a year remodeling it, after it sold, took that profit and bought a small income producing trailer park. (We didn't like the trailer park business but it did make money!) That is how we got started on the first project you see below, the Motor coach.

Since we did not have the cash to buy a fully finished Motor Coach and wanted to travel the US in style like many of the "rich folks" we saw, we decided to buy an old bus shell and put our house remodeling skills to work converting a bus to a beautiful motor coach. Since we had the passive income, it afforded us the time to actually build the bus. It took most of two years and a parking space big enough for it!

Ever wanted to board your own sail boat and set sail for the seven seas?   Me too! So....we found an owner willing to take payments on this beautiful 36 foot Cutter Ketch.

Once again, we used our remodeling skills and sanded the woodwork, refinished the kitchen (galley) and varnished the sticks, (masts). My wife is the best gal I've ever seen at sanding and varnishing woodwork!

@ *HOW* do i buy & own assets?

At the time I didn't know that it's possible to acquire assets without having credit or big savings...

So I decided to TRY to save as much of my income as possible... and then "one day" I'll be able to buy assets that would produce income!

How many of you have tried saving? And what's the problem with this approach?

It takes TOO LONG! It may take a whole life to save a half a million dollars, and by that time the half a million will not be worth much. Just think about it... how much can YOU save every month? How soon will you have a few hundred thousand saved? ... Life is too short for that, in my opinion! My initial approach was the same "WRONG" approach as all my middle-income coworkers.

We all tried to build a financial nest by saving "after-tax" dollars, and then investing this *left-over* into stocks, or mutual funds which we had no real understanding, or control. This is a recipe for disaster.

We all believe that financial planners and advisors, who were working for *their* company, could make us independent of *our* company. Do you see a problem here?

If they knew how to build financial freedom, wouldn't they have been working for themselves, instead of working for a company selling stocks?

Tip: Don't buy individual stocks. Use sectors, spiders, ETFs and other hybrid tools to "play" the market if you must.   For me, the best investments are the ones I can see and feel right in front of my eyes in the form of Real Estate!

@ **Active vs. Passive Income.**

Active income is the one that you EARN – that you work for, regardless if you work for yourself or someone else. Active income comes in only when you work. As soon as you stop, the income stops.

Do you know that most Real Estate investors are earning active income and most stay broke?

They buy, fix and sell properties. Or they flip properties. That is active income.

If you're not sure if that's active income, just ask yourself... *will my income stop if I stop buying and fixing houses?* The answer is yes — your income will stop!

I don't know if you noticed, but that approach is not much different than that of an employee working for a company. I'll tell you what I discovered...

Over the last few years I have travelled extensively to cities throughout the USA and stayed in different cities, all over the country...I consider myself an expert for Pre-Foreclosures, mixed-use buildings, multi-family and Short-Sale investing in many parts of the country.

I'm telling you this to show you that I got exposed to many, many areas and investors out there and what I'm about to share with you has a lot of merit.

◉ **Most investors are working way too hard for the money they make!**

They all look tired and worried about how they are going to find that next deal to pay their bills. That's not "the dream".

They work hard but they are one setback away from being broke. If that one house or a few houses they may have "for sale" don't sell quickly, they are in trouble. *Is that the security YOU are looking for?* I don't think so...

@ An incorrect business model:

Most investors' incorrect model is the primary cause of so much struggling and time wasting. It's sad. It's the reason why an overwhelming majority of people new to real estate investing will fail in achieving their dreams. (Even if they buy lots of courses, study them religiously, and work extremely hard).

"What lies behind us and what lies before us are tiny matters compared to what lies within us." - Ralph Waldo Emerson

Problem #1: The issue is that their business model is based on earning ACTIVE income, and the PASSIVE income component is NOT present at all. In their mind, they are waiting for that day when they'll have enough money saved to buy assets and have passive income. Again this is employee thinking.

Problem #2: They are monetizing only one component of the wealth building ability in Real Estate. They are pre-occupied making the next check so they neglect the other benefits Real Estate investing offers, consequently making it even harder to earn the next check.

I too have been extremely guilty of this model! However, once I got onto these systems that work, I have pursued them with fervor. At one time, I was taking all the profits from any given short sale or construction project and spending them to increase the size of my house, buy a fancier car, purchase a second home and on, and on and on it went. Using the money from the flips and sales to pay payments on non-income producing assets is foolish at best.   It a recipe for disaster!

First Katrina hit all of our properties in New Orleans, stopping any money from sales there for a while. Then the economy took a nose dive, stopping any chance of selling my vacation houses in Florida and other states.   This very efficiently stopped my ability to make the payments on all those goodies.   I took every dime I had in retirement, savings and operating accounts to make payments. *What a waste of good money!* Since my income was based on the equity I had in the houses and sales, I had nothing!

Fortunately I am a fighter, so I wrangled, squirmed, negotiated and used any angle I could find to get the debts and the properties off my back. It took almost 3 years, if you can believe that, but after that, I had liquidated everything without any foreclosures or bankruptcy. Most importantly without a divorce! These types of situations can ruin a marriage; however my wife has been with me every step of the way for almost 30 years and this was no exception.   She hung in there and now we can enjoy building our future, the right way, to include security and freedom!

I tell you this so you will understand that I am speaking from experience and that my knowledge of short-sale, negotiations, creative financing actually saved "my bacon" when it was needed.

I started with nothing and these experiences cost me everything but now you can use those education opportunities to further yourself and save your hard earned money! I did have to start over though, and this time it was using the techniques I talk about here. This is a priceless gathering of information for you to use that will cost you a small amount of time and the cost of this book but will pay you back dividends for years to come.

"Whether you think you can or think you can't, you're right." - *Henry Ford*

Your focus will be putting $10,000, $20,000 or $30,000 into your pocket **as soon as possible** (right?), but you need to REALIZE that it is harder to do that if you neglect the big picture. If you don't leverage ALL the benefits that the Real Estate industry offers, not only that you will never build real wealth, but getting that QUICK CASH will be a lot harder as well!!

If you compare the benefits of *"buying - selling – flipping"* business model vs. *"ownership"* business model, you will find that the only thing the *flipping* model has to offer is profit.   When you look at the *ownership* model you will see that, profit is present as well as, equity build-up through appreciation, equity through depreciation and of course, the tax savings, IRS 167.

As you can see, the *ownership* model utilizes and leverages ALL the components; so obviously building wealth by owning Real Estate is a lot FASTER than "buy-fix-sell" or "flipping" properties, over and over again. Starting from scratch each time... You just need to learn how to OWN without taking risk or at least using *calculated* risk!

Tip: The "ownership" business model that you'll learn about here is not only a faster way to wealth, but it is ALSO a faster way to quick CASH, without the risk or hassles!

@ The Best Business Model for Most

(Your First Million) Let me introduce to you the FASTEST and surest way to your first $MILLION$ —the big picture; and then we'll address how to get to that quick cash within a few short weeks.

I've attended every possible seminar that was available at one time. I've done hundreds of deals and have tried almost every strategy.

AND THEN... one deal made me more money within 30 days, than all of the other deals I'd done up to that time... I'll tell you about it a moment...I've maxed out my credit cards by buying "get rich quick" programs and seminars that never worked... some of you may know the feeling. (I only have one card now, and it's only for emergencies)

Here's what I discovered to be the BEST business model - the quickest and surest way to your first check, and to build a million dollar net-worth in Real Estate as well.

Imagine that there was a way for you to go out and acquire **25** properties within the next year. Let's say these are single-family houses worth **$200,000** each.

If you wonder how you would buy that many houses without using your cash or credit... just know for now that it is possible— it's important that you get the big picture for now.... let's own 25 houses worth $200,000 each...

Let's say you paid **$160,000** for each property. That's only a 20% discount which is very realistic & achievable. (By the way, after you start negotiating full time, you will never again pay full price for Real Estate or many other things, like a rookie amateur investor. You'll know how to buy at a discount!)

Then let's say you place someone in each property that will pay you **$400** above your payment, I'll explain later on how to do that without dealing with tenants (and problems).

And for now, keep in mind that this cash flow is achievable anywhere in the country —we are not talking about rental properties here. I'll explain later.

So, this $400, in our example, is your **Cash Flow** – passive income from day one.

On a $160,000 loan, about **$200** from each mortgage payment will go towards the principal reduction or loan pay-down.
Let's summarize:
25 x $200,000 = $5,000,000 This is the value of your Real Estate portfolio.
25 x ($200k - $160k) = $1,000,000 Your NET-worth (your equity).
25 x 12 mo. x $200 principal reduction = $60,000 This is additional equity after 1y.
25 x 12 mo. x $400 cash flow = $120,000 **Yearly passive income.**
After one year, your NETWORTH (including cash flow) is $1,180,000.
Note: we didn't factor in any appreciation.

Would you feel more secure and free if you had net-worth of over $1M?

Would it make you feel better knowing that someone else is paying down your loan and increasing your net-worth by $60,000+ every year?

If you answered YES to the above questions, you're not alone. Real Estate is cyclical... goes up and goes down. Don't listen to gurus who make you think that the Real Estate will never go up just to sell you their courses.

As we speak, there are already areas in the country that are going up.

"It feels great when you exceed your goals... so think big... you can do it too! It is absolutely possible!" Arnold Goldstein
The hardest part of this whole plan is getting that FIRST property. The second one is a little easier, the third one a lot easier, and after that is sooooo... EASY!
Imagine fulfilling your desires *instead* of just dreaming about them...

When your Real Estate business is making you more money than your current job, you'll have the *freedom* of deciding if you still want to keep it or not.

And in just a few short years, you will build a multi-million dollar net-worth, using a combination of the Awesome Real Estate strategies business models, giving you the ultimate *freedom*!

For now, let's focus on understanding this concept. Because you will be leveraging all the wealth-building components of Awesome Real Estate Strategies, your net-worth will grow exponentially faster as described in this section.

This is called **power of leverage, (leveraging your knowledge, at least)!** And Real Estate is the only investment vehicle that allows this kind of fast wealth building, but only if done the right way. Let's look at the numbers one more time…

Your yearly gain is $60k as loan pay-down, $120k in Cash Flow, and $385k in appreciation. That's total of **$565,000** per year without doing any Active work.

The question is… how many properties do you need to REHAB to make this kind of income in one year? The answer is **too many**! How many do you need to FLIP? The answer is **way too many!**

If an average profit per wholesaling transaction is $3,000 to $6,000, you would need to flip way over 100 properties EVERY year to catch up with the leverage described above. This is why most investors stay poor... they can NEVER catch up.

Tip: **It is easier to buy properties at 20% below their value (below market) than at 40%.**

Obviously, it's a lot easier to buy 25 properties at **20%** discount (which is all you need for our formula to work), than flip 100 properties that you have to put under contract at **30-40%** discount in order for wholesaling to work. Let me make sure you understand this... to get a seller to take a 20% discount the seller doesn't need to be desperate! If that same seller sold their house using a real estate agent, after paying 6% Real
Estate commission, 2-3% closing costs, 2-3% holding cost... they would net only 5-10% more than what they would net by selling to you at 20% discount. What does this mean?

It means that this will work with **more** sellers out there because the 20% discount, we need for our formula to work, doesn't require very motivated or desperate sellers. So, more sellers to work with, the easier it gets and the faster you make money!

This is not the case with other Real Estate formulas, like wholesaling, rehabbing, short sale flips, etc... Those strategies require a lot bigger discount of 30-40% to create profit.

So it's obvious that not every seller will give you 30-40% discount, so you'll have to find a very motivated, if not a desperate seller, to make those strategies work. This means more marketing, more appointments, more work, and fewer opportunities!
Now, I'm not saying you should never do any wholesaling or short sale flips. I do them to this day and they make money.
What I am saying is that those strategies should be part of your "game", but not your main game.

There are deals that will come your way as a result of your marketing or referrals that do not meet this exact business model. In order to monetize those deals we will use the previous Awesome Real Estate Strategies we learned in the first part of the book.
For example, a motivated seller calls me and has a house that needs major repairs.

Since, I am still in the "rehab" business (but you may not want to be because it's too hard), I will attempt to contract the property with a goal to wholesale it, but I know that I can always verify the value and buy it for my next re-hab and sell project... Why not

make some money from the seller who already called, right?

Chapter Nine

Tenant Buyers

"Choose a job you love, and you will never have to work a day in your life." – Confucius

@ **How to structure your Awesome Real Estate business model:**

One method of "Lease purchasing" or "rent to own" is as follows: You are going to put "residents" into your homes, not tenants that will pay you a lot more per month than a tenant, take care of the repairs and never ask for anything.

First, let's talk about buyers and then we will discuss the system for finding sellers. Your buyers will come from running ads on Craigslist, newspapers, signs, business cards and flyers. You will be keeping a "buyers file" with everyone who is interested in "buying" your houses.   They will put some money down, make payments of an amount more than the payments the house has on them now and you will be collecting money not rents. This is not a new concept, but it is still a good one.

These folks are buyers, not renters and if for some reason they walk away, you keep the deposit and do it all over again to make more money. I am including a basic script of what to say when these buyers call.

> "Thank you for calling the ad, (or on our business card or however they found to call you)"
> "What area are you looking for a house?"
> "How much can <u>you afford</u> to put down on your next house?"

Tip: always ask them for a number; do not give them a quote since they may want to put down more than you wanted. I collected a $50,000 deposit once when I was only looking for $10,000!

> "We have several houses coming available in the next few weeks that I think will work for you.   Let me take all your information and follow up with you ASAP."

Finding the houses to buy and funding them.

Many programs promote strategies that are plainly not feasible, may sound good, but don't work. --- ----------That "pollution" may distort or even block you from understanding this business and seeing where the real wealth is.

ⓔ *How can you buy & own Real Estate?*

Take a moment and think about it... HOW? Let me ask you the same question in a different way...You understand that in order to build wealth you need to own Real Estate, but how do you buy it, how do you **fund** it? There are not that many options...

There are really 3 ways to buy Real Estate:

> Using Your CASH

You can use your savings to pay for a property. Most people don't have hundreds of thousands of dollars in their bank account, but even if you do how many properties can you buy? Not 10 or 20... And why would you risk your savings anyway?

> You can go to a bank and get a loan, but that requires good credit and a sizable down payment. Let's say that you had both... The required down payment will limit you to only a few deals. On top of that, the banks will require a personal guarantee making this VERY risky!

I don't know if you realize, but by signing and personally guaranteeing a loan, you are putting in jeopardy everything you own... Do you realize that you are risking your position in life!?! *Why would you ever do that?* If something goes wrong and you can't cover those payments, the bank will foreclose and by doing so they'll most likely incur the loss. By you guaranteeing that loan, you gave them the right to go after you for recovering their loss, ultimately pushing you into bankruptcy!

I can't even begin to describe how many people I've met in my Real Estate career that lost everything by personally guaranteeing loans.

Side Note 1: some of you may be thinking that the way to go is to use the hard money lenders. Absolutely not!

First of all, the financing terms make it impossible to buy and keep properties – it's a short term financing intended for rehabs. The interest rates are way too high to make cash flow from properties cash. Plus, many will also require the personal guarantee! Watch out!

If you prefer that sometimes you can get cash from "private" lenders. That is feasible for a few properties, and on a shorter term of 3 years or less, which you may need in order to build massive wealth.

> And that leaves us with THE LEAST RISKY WAY TO BUY REAL ESTATE...

This is a very smart way to buy properties without taking unnecessary risk!

Using Other People's Credit

It is the foundation of this Awesome Real Estate business Model. We use the "existing" loan that was originated and guaranteed by the seller. This way we don't need to qualify for a loan, our credit doesn't matter, and we are **not** taking the risk by guaranteeing that loan!

This method doesn't require for the loan to be assumable, as I'll explain.

In summary, here are the **advantages**

1. You don't need a down payment when using the existing loan.

2. You don't need your credit.

3. You don't qualify.

4. You don't personally guarantee it.

5. There's little risk.

6. The interest rates are usually low.

7. The supply is unlimited.

Once you learn how this works, you will realize that this is a fun and liberating way to invest in Real Estate!!

I know you may be wondering how this works. Let me tell you, it is so simple that you will be confused by how simple it is. Some people can't even understand it because they are looking for a more complex solution, when, in fact, it is so simple. All you do is get the DEED. When a title company (or an escrow company, or a closing attorney) prepares the deed as part of the regular closing, and once that deed is notarized by the seller and recorded in the county recorder's office, you are the OWNER.

So, once that DEED lists you as a Grantee (the buyer on the deed), and Grantor (seller) has signed it, you are the owner. It does not matter how you paid for that ownership, what the consideration was, where the money came from if any... none of it matters with respect to ownership... if the seller was willing to give you the deed, then <u>you own it!</u>

So, you get the deed and the existing loan stays where it is. I know some of you are asking about if the loan is in foreclosure, so let's look at that scenario.

How do I get a house in foreclosure or behind on payments?

In most cases the seller does not get any proceeds from the sale, but they get the release from the payments. The house is sold and they can move on with their life.

You bought the property without using any money and without ever talking to a bank or a lender, or taking any risk.

If a seller has a lot of equity, then the difference between the purchase price you agreed to and the loan balance will be paid to the seller at closing in cash or in a note (promise to pay at a later date). For example, the house is worth $100,000; the loan is $75,000 and you agreed to pay $80,000. That means that at closing you will be getting the deed "subject to" the existing loan at $75,000 and the seller will be getting $5,000.

In many instances, you will be able to get a seller to agree to take a Note instead of cash at closing, or a portion of both. In this example, the Note will say that you owe $5,000 to that seller, and it will specify the terms of your repayment. Now at this point, you really don't need to think how all this is done because a closing attorney or a title company agent will do it all for you.

IF the folks are behind, you will want to "re-instate the loan" if the numbers work for you.   If they have a second on the property, that's even better since you can usually get the second and the third to take 10%-20% of the balance thus creating equity for yourself and then you re-instate the first. You still have not used any of your own credit.   You may need cash to pay off the second and cash to re-instate the first but if the numbers work, you will get this back from your end "resident buyer".   Thus you can do it all over again!

These "Ingredients "are so simple, why isn't everybody doing it?
The answer is, most people have never heard of it, and most investors don't fully understand it, so they are scared of complications that do NOT exist.
And the truth is... it is simple but only if you use FULL DISCLOSURE from someone who has done it and you use forms from your closing attorney or have your attorney review the forms on our

website. (You get these for free, just go to www.awesomerealestatestrategies.com enter you info and we will email you a PDF with a ton of great forms.

There are steps that you could mess up... like everything else in life. It took me years to figure these strategies out, but when I share them with you, you can go out and do it right away. "Trenches", training for less than thirty bucks, so all of you could have it, it shows you the real-world scenarios of making money. No hype, just Awesome Real Estate Strategies!

If anyone utilizes the strategies here, please, please, please make sure to do what you say you are going to do! If a seller is going to trust you to deed over their house to you, the least you can do, is be honest and try your hardest to keep your word.

Too many investors are using "weasel clauses" to get out of deals and leave the sellers hanging out there. It's just as easy to be upfront about what you want to do and then do it!

NOTES

Chapter Ten

Staying Free and Never Having to "work"

"Choose a job you love, and you will never have to work a day in your life." – Confucius

If you got this far in the book, then you should go to the website. Here's the link: www.AwesomeRealEstateStrategies.com

The fact is... ALL OF YOU reading this book can do this... the beauty is that your situation doesn't matter. The only "ingredient" you need is the seller who is "slightly" motivated, and therefore, ready to take the risk of letting someone else make the payments on the loan, he is liable for.

Tip: Use this script when talking with a seller: "The solution of my buying your house and taking the debt off your back, FAR outweighs the small risk of my not making your payments!"

The truth is, with this method, sellers are at *some* risk of the buyer (you) not making the payments on their loan. You end up with full ownership. They lose all the control, but they are still liable for that loan, and you have no liability.

Sounds unfair? Not really because they would be in a lot worse shape if you didn't step in. So the seller wins as well! Remember the "universal rule", it is - _no one will give up something in life unless they get something in return that they want more._ The **solution** you are providing to them by buying their house outweighs the risk of you not making those payments – the **relief**, a piece of mind, preventing foreclosure, etc. Those "slightly" motivated sellers are all over the place. With this system, you have an unlimited opportunity to build wealth!

It is an awesome way for ALL OF YOU reading this book to start, because YOUR personal situation simply doesn't matter! I hope you're getting excited! Because once you learn how to do this, you will realize there is no reason for you to worry about money!

If your goal is to create massive wealth and completely improve your life, you can do it using this method! When we started, we didn't have much money, or credit. But we had time and energy. IF you dedicate a little time and energy, you will see the results.

Many of you are confused, but that's normal with anyone when a new concept is introduced. But keep reading. This is, in fact, very simple! It has been done many times before, by people like yourself… so just know that YOU TOO can do it! You can profit regardless of your situation!

Awesome Real Estate Strategy example:

Here's an example of a typical deal that can quickly put $25,000.00 into your pocket, give you anywhere between $300 - $700 monthly cash flow, and result in the minimum of $70,000.00 overall profit with no more than a few hours of your time invested. The details:

- 3 Bedroom – 2 Bath House
- Condition – Perfect
- Seller is motivated – purchased another house and can't continue to make double payments. Needs to sell! Not desperate but motivated.
- FMV (fair market value) = $250,000
- Owed on the loan = $200,000 (only one loan @ 5% Interest Rate)
- PITI (principal, interest, taxes & insurance) payment = $1,400/mo.

As the result of your direct response marketing, (see list of marketing at the end of this chapter), the seller called you and asked you for a solution. After asking a few simple key-qualifying questions using the phone script, you determined that there's enough motivation to go and visit the seller.

While on the phone you asked:

Mr. Seller, if an agent brought you a buyer today and the buyer was willing to pay you

$230,000, would you consider that offer?

The seller willingly said "yes" after thinking about his situation and his month's long efforts in selling that resulted in the hassles and still "unsold" house.

At the house, after you've built rapport and credibility, you asked the seller again the same question, now in person:

Mr. Seller, s we were discussing on the phone, If an agent brought you a buyer today and the buyer was willing to offer you $230,000, would you accept that offer?

The seller again answered "yes". And **then** you asked this follow-up question:

Mr. Seller, we learned from working with a lot of sellers, that the sellers are usually very happy if we can get them close to what they would <u>net</u> if they sold it through an agent. If you could <u>net</u> close to what you'd <u>net</u> by selling through an agent, would that work for you?

The seller has already confirmed that in the previous question, but here you asked again in order to setup what follows…
After the seller said "yes", you went together with the seller to calculate what that **net** would be.

Tip: always sit at the kitchen table if possible, not the front room, front porch or anywhere else.   The table puts you at their level and makes them accessible to you.

Now we are going to use a Net-Equity-Worksheet and it "educates" the seller on the cost of the sale and their net amount. It is available on the website:

www.awesomerealestatestrategies.com

Here's the essence of the process. You will deduct the cost of sale from the $230,000 that the seller indicated would be his acceptable price. The cost of sale will amount to between 10-15% depending what you and the seller agreed to include in it. At a minimum, it will include 6% real estate commission, the 3% of closing cost, and 3-4% of holding cost. The holding costs are monthly payments the seller needs to make until he finds the buyer and the buyer buys it.

Let's use 12%, which is a pretty typical number in these types of scenarios. The 12% of $230,000 is $27,600, so after subtracting this amount and the seller's loan balance, the NET to the seller is $2,400.

$230,000.00 -- price the seller indicated would be acceptable minus $27,600.00 – the cost of sale you got the seller to agree to minus $200,000.00 loan balance.

$2,400.00 – NET in the best-case scenario.

After the seller realizes that there is not much profit from the sale, you will ask the seller the following question:

Mr. Seller, in a perfect scenario you would net $2,400. We know that we don't live in a perfect world, so what if we can buy your property for the balance of your loan, would that work for you?

In most cases like this where the seller is **motivated**, and assuming you have built the rapport and credibility properly, the answer will be **YES**! Think about it, why wouldn't they... they are getting close to what they wanted, plus they are MOTIVATED! Worst case, you pay them the $2,400 and the house is yours!

After that you will introduce the "loan staying in their name" concept and get the Purchase & Sale Agreement signed, which will serve as guidance to your closing attorney or the title company to close this transaction.

I have done the above-described process hundreds of times and have very specific presentations that result in high percentages of "YES'" and it makes the whole transaction very smooth. You will want to find the wording that works best for your personality and the sellers you will work with.

Tip: we didn't pressure the seller with *"what's the least you would take?"* **and** *"Is this the best you can do?"* **– Typical crap that kills your deals**.

This "education" process, using the Worksheet, helps the sellers keep their pride, and it doesn't make them feel like they've been taken advantage of. The overall process solves their problem of double payments in this example, and makes you money, a lot of it, as you'll see below.

"The quickest way to double your money is to fold it over and put it back in your pocket." - Will Rogers

"Foreclosure Reversal or loan Re-instatement" allows you to get a deed from a seller in foreclosure, and then send the back payments owed by the seller to the lender. That stops the foreclosure and allows you to own the property with the long term financing. Now that method requires you to have $5,000 to $10,000 in available cash to cover those back payments.

This is a solution to Short Sales that does not require transactional funding, proof of funds, etc. It also doesn't involve "flipping" and all the "red-tape" challenges associated with the "short sale flips". However, it does require $5,000 to $10,000 in cash, but you end up with a long-term financing at a low interest rate, that you are not liable for.

This Awesome R.E. Business Model will allow you to profit without headaches, please answer the following questions:

Do most people out there have perfect credit?

Do most people out there have 20% down payment required to get a loan?

As you realize from these two questions... MOST people out there don't have perfect credit and don't have the 20% in cash for a down payment. The Recession has left a lot of people with damaged credit rating, plus the tight lending guidelines make it very hard if not impossible to get a bank loan.

What does that mean?

It means that if you're selling your houses the same way everybody else is selling them, then you'll get what everybody else is getting… and that is an "**unsold**" house!

The bottom line is… if you are looking for a buyer who CAN get a bank loan, you are selling to minority of people out there. Here's the premise of this business model:

When you can sell properties that most people want to live in, and when you can sell them in a way that most people can afford to buy, then you are fulfilling the need of the majority and consequently, you end up making a lot of money!!

So, while all the homeowners and all the other investors out there are competing for those few buyers with perfect credit and down payment, we'll focus in a totally different direction. We'll act as a "bank" (provide the financing) and sell to people with ANY credit! This is the majority of people out there so our pool of potential buyers will be hundreds of times bigger than our competitions.

This makes your house stand out from all the other houses for sale. Your house comes with "financing"! Because of that…Our houses sell faster and for top price because we have multiple buyers interested in them, instead of the other way around. This results in a faster sale and more profit.

I know you are probably totally confused right now, but this is really simple... here are the basics of how this works...
We will act as a "bank" and provide financing on our own by passing on the existing financing from the previous seller.

In the deal-example given in the previous section, if you remember we purchased the $250,000.00 house for the balance of the existing loan at $200,000.00. Now, if we were to sell that house "outright" using conventional methods, we would net around $25,000.00 or less.

However, would you want to double or triple that profit? Why not? We will double or triple that profit by selling to MAJORITY of people out there with ANY credit and a little down payment... here's how:

We will advertise the house as "No Banks Required – Any Credit Welcome". This will attract hundreds of buyers to call us. When they see an ad where their credit doesn't matter they jump on it right away! So rest assured, you'll get more calls than you can handle! Select the buyer with the largest down payment. Then you will act as a bank, and finance that buyer.

You will use a "wrap" concept that has been used for decades, so you'll have plenty of title companies willing to escrow this type of transactions.

This is the typical outcome for the above deal:

$250,000.00 - Selling price

$25,000.00 - Down-payment received from the buyer (10% is typical for this type of transaction) $225,000.00 is the balance owed to you; that YOU will finance for your buyer. Because the buyer has less than perfect credit, you are entitled to charge a higher interest rate. So, it is very reasonable to ask for 6.95% interest rate, or higher.

Here's your PROFIT based on the existing $200k loan being at 5%, and the new $225k loan being at 6.95%.

- ☝ Up-front profit = **$25,000.00** ... this is from the buyer's down payment
- ☝ Monthly Cash Flow = **$415.74** ... due to difference in the loan amounts and interest rate spread
- ☝ Back-end Profit = **$33,631.10** ... cash you will get when the buyer refinances you after 3 year term.

Your **total profit** taking into consideration the whole deal is **$73,597.32** within a 3-
year term. Not bad for a few hours of work.

@ **Here are 10 strong REASONS why this is the best way to profit today:**

1. You buy without using your credit or money (in most cases). Therefore, you don't depend on the banks or lenders.
2. The financing you "inherit" with the property is at a low interest rate, allowing you to get cash flow from the day one.
3. You are leveraging on the current economic conditions - there are plenty of sellers, who are slightly motivated; or just about to be behind on payments, or already in foreclosure and really motivated.
4. Your product "the house with financing" appeals to the **majority** of people in this economy. You are solving the need and getting paid a lot for doing it.
5. You get top price and the fast sale because most people out there want the "product" you have for sale.
6. Your PROFIT is double or even triple comparing to other investors because you are leveraging multiple properties.

7. You are working SMARTER not harder! You're not rehabbing houses and then hoping to find a buyer who will qualify for the loan (minority). Typical transaction takes 2-3 hours to do.

8. It is easy to delegate. After a few deals, your entire selling process can be delegated. Your entire marketing will be automated, leaving you with a high six or seven figure business that you can run part-time.

9. If the buyer defaults, you get the house back, keep the down payment and do it all over again... get more down payments and additional cash flow. If the house has appreciated, you are the one who benefits from it.

10. You are providing a great service by helping Sellers & Buyers!

What happens if you violate the "due-on-sale" clause?

Nothing! Violating the "due on sale" provision is NOT a crime, and as said above the lenders don't care!

I've bought hundreds of properties this way. Just between my associates, who are practicing investors using these methods, and myself, we've done well over 1,000 of these transactions, and we never had a single lender even ask!

They are happy to get paid!!

What happens if you don't make the payments on the seller's loan?

It's very simple. Don't make promises you can't keep.

In the first few deals, where you're unsure that you can find a buyer, you will be upfront with sellers, and you will tell them that you may not make the payments. You will even have the seller sign a disclosure stating that you're not guaranteeing the payments. Then you have absolutely no liability if you don't make the payments.

I have a special disclosure just for that on the web site.

www.awesomerealestatestrategies.com

Many sellers who are already in foreclosure will agree to that risk.

    © **Due to some new regulations (S.A.F.E. Act), you should be using a loan originator for some of your deals.**

"They had dreams when they were young, replaced by responsibilities as they matured, finally left with nothing but regrets when they're old." Unknown

Some folks just "hope" to be happier. They want to be more successful. But every day is the same, nothing ever changes. They don't feel like they have the time, the discipline, or the resources to take the necessary steps. My whole goal in writing this book was to show you that it's possible. All you need is a desire to learn and implement. And by doing so, you'll put yourself and your family on a path of more enjoyable and fulfilling life... the life without stress and worry about money.

This way, instead of letting life pass you by, you *slam on the brakes* and stop the routine. You stop wishing and waiting, and take a different and more fulfilling alternative route. *All it requires is you to make an effort.* Shortly after your first few deals it will get as easy as you wish it were right now.

Besides, even if it was difficult at first, and even if it took you 6 months to get your first big check (which it won't), **what choice would you have?** Just settle and resign to living an unfulfilling life? Of course not!! A better financial situation isn't going to magically appear out of nowhere, nor are you going to wake up one day and suddenly be living your dream life.

Take the first steps: Start filling your lead funnel with leads.

1. Send out Direct Mailings using foreclosure lists that you either buy or go to the courthouse and get them. Send out mailing s to expired MLS listings if you can get a realtor to send you the list.
2. Use bandit signs everywhere you can put them especially in the key neighbor hoods you want to attract houses and buyers in.
3. Use referrals by contacting real estate agents, mortgage brokers and handing people your business cards.
4. Run ads in Craigslist, and any other online site you think is helpful. Use the nickel ads or local papers or free papers and flyers
5. Pick out the hot prospects and set appointments,
6. Go to people's houses and talk with them. Begin to put together the worksheet with them so they understand who you are and why you will pay what you will pay.

❖ **Locate, Convert and Secure.**

❖ **Present, Educate and Negotiate.**

In closing, I would like to congratulate you on taking the first step to a better future and a more prosperous life.   It takes great courage to reach beyond the normal life and look to other avenues for success. Give yourself a "pat on the back" for allowing yourself the tools to succeed. The strategies outlined in this book will give you a true sense of what is possible within the Real Estate worlds and using one or all of the Awesome Real Estate Strategies I've written about will ensure your success for years to come.

The world of Rehabbing, the system of Short Sales, the Multi-Family investing, Note buying, REO investing, Raising Private Capital and buying without your credit are all going to lead to a Freedom some folks never even dream of having.
Give yourself permission right now, to always dare to dream and always dare to succeed.

Chapter Eleven

Purchasing A Foreclosure At Auction

Foreclosures on residential properties across the country have reached epidemic proportions in recent years, and many experts see a continuing wave of them for the next few years. While those facing foreclosure may find their families uprooted and their financial future uncertain, there are some who will use the opportunity to build their investment portfolio. This could be you! Of course, just because you buy an auction house, does not mean you are making money off someone's heartache, just being a good investor. By buying foreclosed properties through their local court's auctions of homes, condominiums and commercial real estate, buyers and investors stand to build significant wealth.

There are individuals and savvy business entities nationwide whose sole mission is to acquire foreclosed properties at auction. Thanks to the Internet and local municipalities' cataloging of available auction properties – as well as many private sources of reliable information regarding properties coming available on the auction market -- purchasing a foreclosed property through auction has been made easier for those willing to do their homework.

Although it may not be easy, perseverance can be rewarded and profits can be realized by buying up foreclosed properties. You will need to invest some serious time researching your potential investments, and it can get aggressive at times – the faint of heart need not apply.

Getting Started; those who are successful have developed a system to discover, track and evaluate a potential purchase. Most who are serious auction buyers will monitor the local auction websites, and keep statistics on multiple properties simultaneously. The goal is to be ready to bid and buy the minute you have identified a property or properties you feel meet your criteria. If you learn the rules of how the game is played, you can walk away a winner.

Ideally, you should be able to either view the property in person, or through a trusted representative. There are countless details you can learn by simply doing a visual inspection of your potential purchase, the surrounding neighborhood, and other local factors that may determine the value of the property. However, in many cases, there will be little or no access to the inside of a property and a buyer is making the purchase "as is" with no warranty as to its condition.

In Florida, an auction sale of foreclosed properties typically happens within 30-60 days after the foreclosure judgment is entered via court ruling.

In most localities, your county clerk's office will be your primary source of foreclosure property auction details. (They also deal in tax auction sales – make sure you know the difference). The clerk's office will generally publish auction details in the local paper and/or via their website, including a list of properties available, and also the date, time and location of the auction sale proceedings. You need to spend some time familiarizing yourself with navigating the clerk's website in order to best discover properties that are made available, and make the purchase process work for you.

If you plan to attend an auction and bid on a property, you need to be familiar with the process before you show up. Attending a couple of auctions beforehand will give you a sense of the procedures, and provide you with details on how to proceed. The bidding process can vary in different locations – some require certified funds, like a cashier's check – for the entire purchase amount, while others only require a percentage of the total, with the balance being due within a specified number of days. If you have a contact in the real estate business or know an attorney who deals in foreclosure properties, you may want to ask them for input. Yet, nothing is better then being there to see what happens firsthand.

Get the Facts In order to successfully purchase an auction property, there are certain key details you will need to know going in. First and foremost is the realistic estimated market value of the property. You should research recent sales information of similar properties in the same geographic area to determine what the market indicates about the property's actual value. That information, combined with the amounts currently owed and the amounts of any outstanding liens on the property, will help you determine if the property represents a reasonable investment.

There also may be additional fees due to the foreclosing lender, so make sure you are aware of all applicable costs before you bid.

The opening bid amount represents the total of all monies owed on the property. In some cases, the winning bidder will be responsible for satisfying any outstanding liens on the property before a certification of title transfer will be issued. An attorney, Real Estate Title Company or a search of county records will unearth any liens that have been placed on the property. Be sure to do a thorough search for outstanding liens – there may be more than one mortgage on the property, and could be liens which have been levied on a secondary mortgage, or a tax lien, in place.

Even after the auction, a tax lien could still be in effect, so make sure you understand the total financial obligations you will face in order to legally take possession of the property. You should also factor in any potential repair or updating costs that may be needed to bring the property up to a reasonable market value, if your intent is to either re-sell it or rent it out as an investment property.

The foreclosing lender will typically bid $100 (to keep doc stamps low). If there are no other bids above the total amount owed, the foreclosing lender will obtain possession of the property. Working in your favor is the fact that in the vast majority of cases, the lender does not want the property, and is anxious to see it sold successfully at auction.

How Much To Bid? Once you have all the facts, you will need to determine the specific amount you can comfortably bid in order to justify the purchase as a reasonable bargain. It is vital that you resist the temptation of falling in love with a property you are planning to bid on. In the heat of an auction setting, where there will likely be multiple bidders vying for the same property, it is easy for your emotional attachment to get the better of you, and you may wind up bidding more than the amount you set as your limit. This is only bricks and mortar, after all, so try to keep your wits about you. With the prevalence of foreclosed properties hitting the auction market these days, you can be reasonably assured that, should you not walk away with the property you planned on buying, there will be a similar opportunity coming along right behind it.

Obviously, you need to be certain you can complete the transaction if you end up being the successful bidder. Make sure you have sufficient available cash with which to close the deal in the specified time frame after the sale — in most cases, you will lose any deposit you paid at the auction should you be unable to finalize the deal. Remember — this arena is not for novice investors.

Ready, Set, Go... Once you have all your research done and your facts understood, you are ready to jump in and bid. Each auction will be under the direction of a trustee who has been appointed by the foreclosure court. You need to know how to contact that person, in order to verify if the auction you plan on attending is still scheduled. Often, last minute schedule changes or other factors will dictate a change of the actual auction date. It is suggested to call a day in advance to double-check.

In Miami-Dade County, The Clerk of Courts now conducts an online version of foreclosed property auctions. Those who register in advance via their website can place bids online, as opposed to actually attending the auction. But, be warned — this method is generally only recommended for those experienced bidders who are intimately familiar with how the process works.

If you would rather be on-site when the auction takes place, plan on getting to the physical auction location early. Hopefully, you will have had the experience of attending a few auctions as an observer already, so you should be comfortable with the atmosphere. Just keep in mind, there will be people there who do this for a living, and take it very seriously. Don't be surprised if you are not welcomed with open arms by the other bidders – remember that they will most likely be competing with you to snatch up the same property, and some of them don't exactly welcome competition.

But, don't let them intimidate you. Again, keeping your composure and your emotional (and financial) wits about you is the key to walking away the happy owner of a potentially rewarding piece of real estate.

Congratulations! There are some follow-up steps you will need to do in order to successfully take ownership of the property once you have become the successful bidder. Be sure to get all the pertinent documentation you require from the auctioneer to indicate you are the winning bidder, and clarify any additional measures necessary to take possession of the property. It may be smart to consult with an experienced real estate attorney if you have any questions about legal requirements concerning the transfer of title.

Depending on the local laws, you may have legal rights to the property immediately, or it may be up to 30 – 60 days. There may also be what is called a "redemption period", within which the former owner has a chance to buy the property back from you, providing they have paid the full auction amount plus any applicable costs and fees. This rarely happens, though – chances are that if the property was sold at auction, the former owner is in no position to buy it back. Yet, you would be smart to hold off on any planned improvements to the property until you are absolutely certain it is yours.

If there are tenants currently residing in the property, you may need to evict the tenants. You should consult with a lawyer familiar with the process, or contact your local sheriff's office to learn how to do it legally, and as efficiently as possible. Of course, you may also elect to allow the tenants to remain in the property, if even for a short period, which could help you recoup some of your initial outlay of funds used in the purchase process.

Buying a foreclosed property through an auction can be an excellent way to build your real estate portfolio, providing you are aware of all the potential pitfalls along the way. Smart investors make substantial profits using this acquisition method, and treat it as a business operation. Arm yourself with as much information as possible in order to make an educated decision, and you can find that the efforts are well worth your time and hard work. Do your best to avoid "analysis paralysis" since it will keep you on the side lines longer than any challenge an potential property will, also, keep smiling and making friends.

One of my mentors in the car business, Jay Calendar, told me a long time ago *"you'll rarely do business with your enemies, our friends want to do business with us, so make friends!"*

And last but not least, don't listen to anyone who's broke!

Credits

(1)...Carlton Sheets: known on TV and Media for his Real Estate Investment Strategies.

(2)...Ron LeGrande: a millionaire who has helped many people achieve the financial freedom and fulfill their dreams.

(3)... Jeff Kaller: "Mr. Preforeclosure" and an expert on foreclosures. He is working on sustainable communities and education.

(4) ...Short Sale System: A compilation of several studies of the current banking short sale system and in no way affiliated with an individual's courses or instructions unless coincidentally.

(5).....Marco Rubel. An instructional leader who provides housing solutions for families who need a helping hand.

Index

About the Author

Shawn M. Tennefoss is an active Real Estate investor, General Contractor and Expert Negotiator.

Shawn lives with his wife, Kathleen, in Sunny South Florida, (SoFLo) and Vibrant, Lively New Orleans, Lousiana, (NoLa). The couple has been featured for the TV series "Flip that House" while rebuilding their properties in New Orleans after hurricane Katrina.

It has been said that Shawn is involved in Real Estate in the "tri-coastal" regions of the USA, The East Coast, West Coast and Gulf Coast. This wide sweeping regional experience has given Shawn a perspective and knowledge that is invaluable within the real estate arena.

Shawn, with the assistance of his wife, Kathy have worked in every aspect of the Real Estate business, including hands on rebuilding/renovations, short sales, quick flips, wholesaling, bank owned, note purchases, marketing, retailing, owner financing, and so much more.

When Shawn talks with you about his experiences, he is speaking firsthand about the work involved in making money, the ethics and the knowledge required to become wildly successful in the world of "Awesome Real Estate Strategies".

Some of his favorite places to travel include; Key West, Florida, New Orleans, Louisiana, Denver, Colorado, Portland, Oregon, Paris, France, and Holly Colorado. Through Real Estate and the freedom it provides, Shawn and Kathy are able to travel to the parts of the world they love and still maintain a comfortable income.

"All the best!"

NOTES

NOTES

Made in the USA
Columbia, SC
30 July 2018